Harvey Molotch   Davide Ponzini   photography by Michele Nastasi

Seeing through Gulf Cities
Urbanization in and from the Arabian Peninsula

Doha, 2017 (previous pages)
Looking North
from the Old Town

Doha, 2017
West Bay
from Skyline Observation Point

Seeing through Gulf Cities

Urbanization in and from the Arabian Peninsula

Harvey Molotch
Davide Ponzini

photography by
Michele Nastasi

with an afterword by
Nasser Rabbat

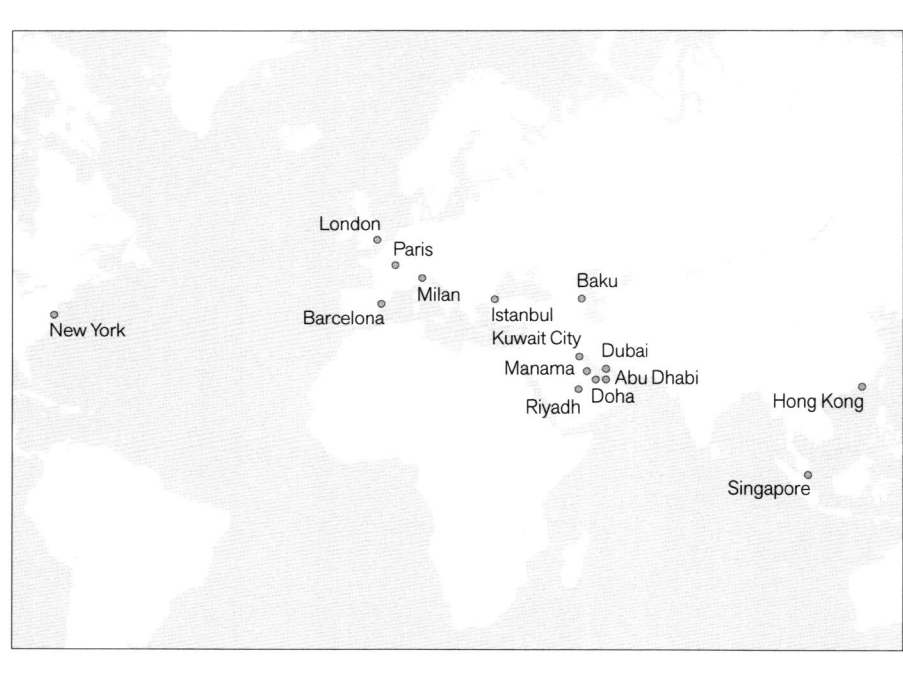

Contents

11 Introduction
    **Learning from
    (and through) Gulf Cities**

25 Report from the Photographer
    Gulf Cities as Lens
    Michele Nastasi

36 **See the Gulf, See the World**
54 **City Icons for the World**
68 **Tourist City as Hub**
78 **Buildings Travel**
90 **Landmarks Can't Travel**
106 **Testing and Spreading**
116 **Collecting Trophy Buildings**
128 **Spaces of Workaround**

141 Afterword
    **From Trade Cities to Traded
    Cities in the Arabian Gulf**
    Nasser Rabbat

154 Appendix
    Post-its from the Gulf

168 References

170 Acknowledgments

Abu Dhabi, 2017 (next pages)
View from Al Reem Island

Abu Dhabi, 2012
Façade Cleaners

Introduction
Learning from (and through) Gulf Cities

Harvey Molotch
Davide Ponzini

Looking for Gulf Cities

Gulf cities startled us – so much wealth, so many buildings, with social and economic arrangements hard to quite understand. As we began our 'Learning from Gulf Cities' initiative in the mid-2010s, we knew the theories and explanations of urban growth and transformation we had at hand, mostly based on Western histories and realities, would not get us very far. Motivated by ignorance, we started to look for new ways to think and indeed to see. Of course, we knew to beware taking refuge in some updated orientalism, basking in some postmodern exotic. Nor should we focus on lacks (like of voting) or excess (like of luxury). Instead, we aimed, as strategic epistemology, at the how – just how do the disparate elements, many of them indeed unfamiliar, combine as configuration, as a viable assemblage of social, architectural, and political reality.

Rather than moralistic classification – good or bad, futuristic or backwards – we had to learn the reality of the interstices: there it is, but where are the ligaments that meet-up, that connect one part with the other, that hold it together. And as a further 'how,' we wanted to know the ways these cities (and city-states) connected to other urban places. Following up, we could also see Gulf-based fluxes of investment and architectural schemas launching to other cities in the Middle East, Asia, and the Western world. Increasingly, we could see that our studies of the Gulf provided clues about contemporary urbanism operating across the world; Gulf cities were our sites, but not analytic ends in themselves.

Beyond our own capacities of discipline and national experience (Molotch as US sociologist, Ponzini as Italian urban scholar), we came to involve twenty colleagues from relevant backgrounds, some with deep knowledge of the Middle East. We gathered in a series of workshops, seminars, and public events in the Gulf, in New York, and Milan. Our founding consensus was to empirically learn from Gulf cities, minimizing preoccupations from prior intellectual commitments. The various contributors, some eminent in their fields, some newly emergent, authored separate chapters for our edited volume published in 2019, *The New Arab Urban*.[1] In our ongoing intention to neither celebrate nor deplore our Gulf cities, we were echoing Robert Venturi, Denise Scott-Brown, and Steven Izenour's 1970s classic about a US desert city with similarly mixed reputation and much to teach, *Learning from Las Vegas*.[2]

A pervasive problem all Gulf scholars face is limited access to information and data of the sort routinely available for places elsewhere in the world. Although some key actors in real estate and public agencies were generous with time and information, we found it difficult to connect with decision-makers in any systematic way. Interviewing, site-visits, and ethnographic mapping were restricted (although now starting to loosen up). Formal approval could be gained for visits to sites, but in some cases, like worker residential camps, it was, and remains, impossible. Databases about cities, their populations and economies do exist, but they have only recently been made (unevenly) available.

From official circles, the guiding principle is to create positive impressions. A few critical scholars working locally have managed to stitch together bits of information, some resting on publicly-available data. But in the main, government functionaries, media figures, or academic leaders risk opprobrium if they speak out candidly. At the starting point, dissatisfaction with inherited conceptual toolboxes and a general shortage in information combined to push us toward an approach that was, at least in part, new to us.

---

[1] Molotch, H., & Ponzini, D. (2019, Eds.). *The New Arab Urban. Gulf Cities of Wealth, Ambition, and Distress*. New York: New York University Press.

[2] Venturi, R., Brown, D. S., & Izenour, S. (1972). *Learning from Las Vegas: The Forgotten Symbolism of Architectural Form*. Cambridge MA: MIT Press.

Follow the Buildings!

Although the speed of change and paucity of data created challenge, buildings could let us in. They provide evidence of larger political, social, and cultural dynamics. Buildings undeniably exist, and even in the Gulf, maybe especially in the Gulf, they are documented in publicly-accessible real and virtual media. They are often celebrated by their sponsors who showcase architectural prowess, experimental technologies, and financial capacities. Designers, investors, developers, and even government officials hope to make the news through these works. Particularly if they have residential, hotel, or upmarket retail elements, the projects are massively advertised, making evident their target markets and envisioned fit with local amenities and public conveniences. For us, they provide data.

Greatly enriching our endeavor was our deep dive into architectural photography that the buildings' physical presence provides – on the horizon, in real time, and as investment vehicles. Key to broadening our thinking and method has been collaboration with the architectural photographer and scholar, the widely admired Michele Nastasi. His work came to serve as platform for an innovative combination of photography and social research. Linked into our Gulf initiative already under way, Nastasi in 2017 embarked on an extensive photographic mission in Abu Dhabi, Doha, Dubai, Kuwait City, Manama, and Riyadh. Complementary to his previous work (some of it also in collaboration with Ponzini), Nastasi broadened beyond conventions of architectural photography – given as they are to treating buildings as significant sui generis, monuments to a designer's prowess. Such icon-making bleaches out context, both physical and social.

Celebratory of architects and their patrons, the resulting images conceal the urban clutter, layers of urbanistic adjustments, and bodily presences of real city life. Nastasi's pictures, at least when they are not commissioned by architectural firms and magazines, don't do this. They intentionally make visible what happens in front of buildings, behind them, and adjacent. The captured acts and artifacts are thus made into parts of a city, region, and the world.

Urban Photography in Iterative Method

Although there are rich photographic traditions in fields like visual anthropology and visual sociology, urban and architectural studies tend to use photographs in more limited and formulaic ways. Sometimes, the picture is in secondary position, used to illustrate an aspect of the story being told with words. The alternative, as in architecture books (coffee table-bound), elevates the image itself as the main point. Architecture is itself the focus, with artistic tactics – angles, lighting, and sight lines – mobilized to enhance tribute. Whether in the form of exhibitions, compendia, off-prints, books, or web sites, photography provides a didactic visualization of a preformed argument.

In our case, working with Nastasi, photography is co-equal to the story and intrinsic to its development. Rather than being the ghosts that are themselves off-camera – acknowledged with a credit line in a caption or appendix – here the photographer is full-on partner. For us, compared to both social science and architectural photography, the photograph is both less of the story and more of it. It is less because of our parallel efforts at carrying out interviews, data collection, and continuous interaction with colleagues. But it is also made essential because, even as combined, knowledge from usual social science sources and theories is incomplete – in the Gulf region especially – and strongly in need of augmentation.

Photographs had to do more for us because of the limits the local regimes placed on what could be known. Our images had to give us clues of what else we needed to do. The bric-a-brac made visible in a Nastasi image of an otherwise glamorous building gives off questions for further inquiry. We could point to details and ask colleagues about what we were noticing, and ask them about what we were failing to notice, a version of photo elicitation technique.[3] We could learn more about provenance – of a truck, a shovel, a window washer, and the dust on a uniform. As sociologist-photogra-

[3] Collier, J. Jr. (1967). *Visual Anthropology: Photography as a Research Method.* New York: Holt, Rinehart, Winston.

[4] Page 12, Becker, H. S. (1974). 'Photography and sociology.' *Studies in Visual Communication*, 1(1), 3-26; see also: Becker, H. S. (1995). 'Visual sociology, documentary photography, and photojournalism: It's (almost) all a matter of context.' *Visual Sociology*, 10(1-2), 5-14, and the photo-ethnographies of Douglas Harper: Harper, D. (2006). *Good Company: A Tramp Life*. New York: Routledge; Harper, D. (1987). *Working Knowledge. Skill and Community in a Small Shop*. Chicago: University of Chicago Press.

pher Howard Becker once explained about such tactics: 'I'm not referring to anything very esoteric, just to the procedure which allows you to make use of what you learn one day in your data-gathering the next day.'[4] The technique is to show the pictures to people who know the situations under study and elicit from them explanations and suggestions of other things that need to be photographed, analyzed, and so on.

Better known, of course, is the use of the photograph in social and political rhetoric, tellingly against child labor, destitution, and repression. Photographs aid environmental reform, documenting ecological loss and, as with the blue dot image of earth taken from outer space, inspiring unity and agreements. In such endeavors, the photographer is not just a witness, but partner in knowledge-making. For our part, the relative paucity of usual forms of documentation pushed us to find other ways to learn – and reminding once again of the authoritarian sociopolitical regimes that were both responsible for bringing the projects to fruition and also for inhibiting elaboration of how it had been done.

Perhaps most ambitiously, photography could depict transnational interconnectedness, of projects, of designers, and of outcomes. Pictures are static – 'stills' – but in series can reveal emulation, duplication, and efforts at distinction. Looking them over, we could see transnational travel and spread. Images of urban projects by the same designer (or even a different one) helped make evident the nature of how design travels from one place to another, including the adaptations made along the way. To help the process, we mounted images as diptychs and triptychs to compare a similar design concept as realized in different environments. We could see, for example, how a building on an open plaza in Barcelona, filled with pedestrians coming and going, is a different 'work' than the same architect's formally similar building in Doha's people-free business district. Sidewalk liveliness or lack of it, similarly changes architectural result. And it also shows different versions of urbanistic rectitude – what

Abu Dhabi, 2017 (next pages)
View of Saadyiat Island and the NYUAD Campus
from Al Reem Island

authorities tolerate or restrict (push carts? hanging out? sport?). The contrasting versions of order and disorder are inscribed for inspection.

Thanks in part to Nastasi's non-Gulf work – pictures he made before and during his efforts with us – we could further incorporate New York, Paris, London, Barcelona, Milan, Singapore, Istanbul, and Baku as sites to learn from. Supported by textual evidence and an expanding library of images, we could make our pointed comparisons. So when we found, for example, two 'matched' waterfront complexes in Abu Dhabi and London, we could compare their development processes. We could dig into the buildings as data, striving to uncover processes that cause the traveling buildings to land differently in their respective locations. Knowing that the same UK-based firm designed both, then led us to map all the completed projects of that firm around the world, available to us as web-based images. In still further follow-up, Nastasi visited a Baku (Azerbaijan) complex – in the same design idiom and again by the same firm – further elaborating the travel story.

As per general procedure, the photos provide information; our data follow-ups confirm, disconfirm, or further elaborate what the photo might indicate. Shot by shot, topic by topic, we could document transnational trajectories. Round after round, text after text, the process continues, altering what we know. This is neither deduction, nor induction, but abduction – likely the most common (if not always acknowledged) method of learning in both science and everyday life.[5] It is an open, shifting way of understanding. As evidence evolves, alternatives can be posed and best overall reckoning come to be (conditionally) accepted. As with other modes of abduction, having diverse and even inconsistent kinds of evidence becomes an asset, not a trouble.

5
The founding doctrine is from Charles Peirce. See Hartshorne, C., Weiss, P., & Burks, A. (1931, Eds.). *Collected Papers of Charles Sanders Peirce*, Cambridge MA: Harvard University Press.

Seeing through Gulf Cities in this Book

Since early in our work together we have had an eye on public inclusion, to be accomplished primarily through public exhibitions – in Abu Dhabi and New York. Exhibitions do not tolerate long texts, obscure references or – God forbid – footnotes. So we needed to condense findings and come up with effective images. Along with intermediate workshops among experts and colleagues, the exhibition responses tested and elaborated our methods. As with others involved in the project, visitors could point to the photos and pose questions; we tried to be on the scene and parried answers. Partly in response to what people were saying and asking, we added in (and corrected!) maps and infographics – charts, diagrams, and the like. The hard deadlines of exhibition schedules, while limiting the number of creative loops we could run, intensified and accelerated the process.

The medium of exhibition, with which neither of us had much prior experience, generates different kinds of demands than writing articles, books, or running a classroom. Compared to our usual practice, we had lost control. At the gallery, people spend as much or as little time as they want at any given image or information panel. Although we did our curatorial best to channel our audience with cues as to what to see and in what order, visitors go their own way, without regard to our intended sequencing. People can start in the middle or at the very end; it is up to whim. Small children may escape their parents, ending up who knows where. And, for all, there are bodily needs for food and toilets that interrupt, as well as serendipitous encounters with friends. The organizers need more than a good game plan; their materials have to be rugged enough to do their job no matter what.

This book contains some of what survived, readapted now for print. Infographics and images are based on the exhibition works and on the relevant sources of information included for each image where appropriate. In addition to what had been on exhibition walls, we added more photographs from Nastasi's archive. We edited texts as appropriate. Boiled down and also extended, our work results in the eight following chapters.

Our first chapter – namely 'See the Gulf, See the World' – introduces the region as we came to know it. Bypassing archetypal assumption of the West as 'leader' – the source of knowledge and initiatives that have consequence in the East – we look to the Gulf for harbingers of what may be coming to more established urban centers. Expressed often as complaint, a repeated catechism heard in cities like London is that a given building is 'too Dubai.' Perhaps. But one of the teachings from the Gulf, as it turns out, is that spectacularization attracts media attention, tourism, and investment. Even when making little sense from a land-efficiency standpoint, an isolated skyscraper seems to attract buyers as well as visitors – as described in our second chapter, 'City Icons for the World.' In the third chapter 'Tourist City as Hub', we examine more broadly how using design and other devices of attraction leverage an increasingly large share of international air traffic. The Gulf has become not only a global node, but a destination. The nature of its tourism reflects capacity to create cities as consumption artifice almost sui generis – camel races, Versailles-scaled mosques, ski slopes inside shopping malls in the desert, and abounding opulence.

The chapters 'Buildings Travel' and 'Landmarks Can't Travel' hone in on contemporary Gulf architecture – as being made real in the region. There is some – but not much – deference to the punishing sun and ambient sand. Largely absent are formerly common clichés of an exotic east. Instead, the showing off bespeaks – and advances – urban and architectural spectacle. The architects and sheikhs have apparently also, in their way, learned this from Las Vegas and took it to a high – transnational – level.

In this and other respects, Gulf cities function as urban 'test beds' for architectural, engineering and design experiments that developers then export and adapt elsewhere in the Middle East and beyond – a theme taken up in chapters 'Testing and Spreading' and 'Collecting Trophy Buildings.' The international mobility of Gulf-based real estate operatives and investors is crucial in the travels. We see it in the design set-ups and glean some of the details from the less-guarded interviews with informants – developers, civic officials, and architects among them.

Finally, in our last chapter 'Spaces of Workaround' we attend to the city of Abu Dhabi, the oil-enriched capital of the UAE. As with similar evolutions in other parts of the Gulf, it has developed special zones and rule-making exceptions, exemptions, and incentives that help bypass fiscal, religious and social constraints. This too perhaps is harbinger of tilt toward an adaptive global capitalism that omits, when expedient, democratic governance – even from mention. A convenience of Gulf city studies, the manifestations become clear through singularity of decision-making and capacity for deliberate enactment. On the cityscape, we see the ideas and designs from multiple origins get assembled, tested and then, as opportunity presents, rapidly move to other regions. We watch as policies and projects bypass local frictions to find their own culturally and politically specific money-making niche. In its way, the Gulf is its own kind of globalism lab.

We imagine this book as an invitation, based on studies wherever, to refine, elaborate, or contradict our findings, as well as the specific utility of our visual-analytic method. The trick is to cross disciplinary as well as geographic boundaries to see urban connections as they continue to emerge. We hope this book will inspire further urban seeing, on and off the beaten track, as scholars, practitioners and those who make pictures take up the never-ending task.

Riyadh, 2017 (next pages)
View from King Abdullah Financial Center

Dubai, 2017
JBR Beach

Report from the Photographer
Gulf Cities as Lens

Michele Nastasi

Seeing, for photographers, is a magic word; the visual runs – one way or another – as common thread through all they do. However obvious it may be that photographers see, it is not certain what they see, and what they will be able to render visible to others. The agenda is wide open; selectivity, at every step, is necessary. The series of photographs of architecture and landscapes collected within these pages is one such result, and here I reflect on just how it has happened.

Whatever pretense to objectivity may influence common thinking of how photography works, no such simple reductivity played a role either in the making of my images or the thinking of my colleagues in our Gulf cities initiative. We well understood that seeing something of reality depends on many intertwined elements, including, first and foremost, one's own personal experience of the world. The pretense of objectivity adds nothing and indeed narrows the range of what can be seen, represented, or – down the line – appreciated.

Visualizing Discoveries

When the academic world calls me an 'artist,' I sense – even when expressed admiringly – a suspicion of unreliability. It works off a stereotype of the 'creator' as a self-absorbed autonomous individual, a searcher of truth perhaps, but subject to excessive self-referentiality. Producing trustworthy knowledge of the real world should be guided by objective methods and outcomes, like science. Scientific research and the practices that produce images are – as stereotype – distinctly separate domains, which do not usually share understanding of the other's aims and means. In part, this understanding – or misunderstanding as I think it truly is – has not always been so prevalent. At least until the eighteenth century, the worlds of research and art were more fundamentally synthetic. Truth-seekers, of whatever sort, did not ignore in-depth visual perception as tool and goal. Images and optical devices were readily utilized in methods of investigation and dissemination, and appreciated accordingly. The aesthetic and the scientific were conjoint.

With the rise of empiricism in the West, a certain vigilance took hold against the seductive fictions of the *Ancien Régime* and its accompanying self-serving mystifications. Oral and visual culture could be associated with deception and irrationality. The 'merely' aesthetic would, in progressive ideology, need to be supplanted by systematic studies reported from unbiased perspective – documented and communicated through a prioritization of text, not imagery.[1] But all along, of course, the separations were not clear-cut, and indeed mutual learnings were taking place, albeit sometimes in subtle ways.

Also at work was a world of expanding travel and exploration, the Middle East region being itself the great storied crossroads. Geographic expansions fostered new aesthetics that drew on observation, rather than classical naturalism or religiosity. These trends gave rise to new ways of producing and valorizing images.[2]

To cite a foundational case of modernizing world-making, the painter William Hodges worked for three years on Captain Cook's second voyage aboard the ship *Resolution* (1772-1775), commissioned by the British Admiralty and the Royal Society. His sketches documented places and peoples encountered by the great expedition. On return to London, Hodges completed many of his landscape oil paintings, some at large scale. The results were not only topographical, but pictorial and markedly expressive. He created images for the European 'experimental gentlemen,' interested not in problems of taste but in gathering, classifying, and interpreting information. But taste, inevitably was attended to and indeed generated attention.[3]

---

[1] Stafford, B. M. (1994). *Artful Science: Enlightenment Entertainment and the Eclipse of Visual Education.* Cambridge MA: MIT Press.

[2] Stafford, B. M. (1984). *Voyage into Substance: Art, Science, Nature, and the Illustrated Travel Account, 1760-1840.* Cambridge MA: MIT Press.

[3] Smith, B. (1992). *Imagining the Pacific. In the Wake of the Cook Voyages.* New Haven: Yale University Press.

Subsequently, photographers developed their own ways of seeing, combining documentary, scientific, and illustrative approaches adding to ideals from fine-art painting. They utilized a personal and interpretative approach to be sure, but one aligned with the technology and specific aesthetic potential of the new medium. In the second half of the nineteenth century new subjects come into view. That meant 'discovery' of the Middle East and Asia could happen through sensibilities and evolving tools of European photographers. There was documentation of monuments and architecture as well as proto-anthropological examination of other peoples and their artifacts.

Roughly coincident, American photographers could represent territories of the West, still largely untouched by Western civilization and the social-ecological consequences to come. In making visible the geographical, naturalistic, and geological aspects of those vast places, these photographic pioneers shaped a powerful iconography of imperial drive, but also giving rise to a national system of parks and wildlife protection. Along the way, they (and their successors) documented nascent urban settlement, the work and lives of miners and railway crews, and significant archaeological finds and ethnographic detail. Among the still-treasured images are views of the arid regions in Nevada, Arizona, and New Mexico by Timothy O'Sullivan, spectacular landscapes of Carleton E. Watkins and Eadweard Muybridge on Yosemite, to name a few of the most well-known.[4]

Today's Gulf cities were not, at least not in the same sense, unexplored territories. But their rapid and radical development, as well as the wide expanses of open space, provide some ichnographic similarity with something so otherwise different as the American West. As an author of images, I situate myself with those who participated long before me, particularly those depicting landscapes and the struggles for livelihood in which they occurred. There are both similarities and differences among the historical examples, but always balancing aestheticization and realism – a continuity in the history of representation with which I identify.

Dubai, 2017 (next pages)
Sheikh Zayed Road

---

[4] Naef, W. J., & Wood, J. N. (1975). *Era of Exploration: The Rise of Landscape Photography in the American West, 1860-1885.* Buffalo: Albright-Knox Art Gallery and The Metropolitan Museum of Art.

Where the Urban Takes Place

Photographing architecture in the contemporary Gulf comes with its own particularities. In the race to build the hyper-modern, there is little mystique of indigenous genius insulated from 'outside' trends and concerns. The most prominent contemporary buildings in the Gulf are clearly based on recipes of iconic architecture as globally circulated, with foreign architectural firms prominently (and pridefully) featured. The canon of abstraction, as global and 'world-class' trend, manifests as formal exercises, arranged on a taken-for-granted emptiness of desert 'tabula rasa.' Capacity for a media-ready image is built-in from the buildings' first concept. Here promotional representation of architecture is not only possible but is itself promoted. The buildings are 'creations' of wonder. Grouped as skyline, they form a collection of icons – easy-to-use images that serve the interests of both the local regime and global architects. It is perhaps its own category of the sublime, facilitated by intersecting bigness: the desert and infrastructure gigantism, distinct from human bodies and mundane artifacts. The irony of such photographic practice is that the cities themselves – as ways of life and sustenance – are eclipsed; urban lives in places like Dubai, Abu Dhabi, and Doha are largely rendered invisible.

    For me, deference to these conventions sacrifices a great potential of photographic practice. While the skyline as the subject of a photograph can denote grandeur and business friendliness, it shows little of the actual places. So, to both understand and represent, I take a step back from the most persistent 'scenic' structures and look for goings-on at the base of the buildings, and for the niches where people find respite from weather, isolation, and tedium. They are complexly configured, not only with urban bric-a-brac but also the human beings who come, go, and stay. Making this reality visible involves showing everything that constitutes the landscape, including sand and those elements too often eliminated from the frame for being insufficiently photogenic. Or because they are, in direct or indirect ways, seen as threatening to political structures or marketing prospects.

In Gulf cities, the most 'forbidden' subjects are people. In part this prohibition springs from a different cultural conception of privacy, one that makes the human figure problematic as photographic subject. Religion eschews human representation. There are also difficulties that arise from images that depict troubling aspects of the larger social and political framework from which the scenes arise. The workers who erect and maintain buildings and infrastructures are not shown. Their working and living conditions have become topics of intense discussion in the West. The 'wrong' revelations risk loss of access to the country. There is always a temptation to anticipate disapproval and engage in self-censorship.

In photographing the Gulf cities, I try to get it all in. I aim to balance different elements rather than just foregrounding one single aspect, one particular building or some composition of them. What I see through my lens is a wide field where the urban takes place. Instead of only seeing from high above (a regular point of view which photographers inherited from Romanticism), I shoot from ground level where I can intermix with inhabitants on foot. I am well accustomed to walking and to the human scale, which leads to proximity and realism. I think this better embraces the complexity of all urban places. Perhaps this proclivity derives from the urban life of a European – and an Italian in particular. I leave renditions of fantastical buildings – monumental in height, jagged in form – for other purposes.

The wide field of the Gulf invites – another irony here – a more open photographic agenda. In other cities, where most every space has been occupied, cleared, and built on repeatedly, the past has long gone. In the Gulf, new buildings unfold where no permanent structures have been present. One can see the old-built, the new-built, the being-built (with adverts and fences), and the still-to-be-built – a city as fast-track history, almost as itself an ongoing construction site. Through the Gulf lens, the ever-emergent city is more legible as fact.

For me, the goal is always to involve an appropriate audience in new appreciation of the complexities. The task is to create images without sentimentality, bellicosity, or overt aestheticization. Avoiding simplistic confrontation, photographic practice can be the starting point for frank discussion of even controversial topics. It is a means to configure connective tissue not only between diverse actors and artifacts, but also between different intellectual fields and cultural adherences.

Seeing through this Book

Bolstering interdisciplinary orientations, visual studies in recent decades increasingly have opened discussion of how images add value across intellectual realms.[5] In architecture and urban planning, the visual has long been intrinsic to research and professional practice, of course. But the visual also has had presence in other domains, including anthropology and sociology, as evidenced by my collaboration with the sociologist and urban planner with whom I have worked so closely on this and prior initiatives. Conversations and questioning across diverse fields have structured how images were gathered, interpreted, and used to stimulate still further inquiries. With such border-crossings across realms, there is prospect for rethinking the nature of places – of buildings, their uses, and their users. Photography, in particular, is a practice that feeds on exchanges with other disciplines. Results, as presented in these pages, are thus methodologically experimental, with interdisciplinarity an intrinsic element. As with our exhibitions and mock-ups, held in three different countries, this book continues a learning enterprise.

An earliest group of photographs derives from 'Starchitecture,' the research I conducted with Davide Ponzini beginning in 2008, which compared the iconic architectures of Abu Dhabi, New York, and Paris, with one

[5] Elkins, J. (2003). *Visual Studies. A Skeptical Introduction*. New York: Routledge. See also Elkins, J., & Naef, N. (2011, Eds.). *What is an Image?* University Park: Pennsylvania State University Press.

another as well as with certain sites elsewhere. Some of these images were taken during photo shoots commissioned by architects and magazines, while others derive from efforts on my own. In broader terms of collaboration, my artist residency at the Akkasah Center for Photography at New York University Abu Dhabi (NYUAD) in early 2017 was of primary importance. During this period I was able to work in the six Gulf cities presented here (Abu Dhabi, Doha, Dubai, Kuwait City, Manama, and Riyadh). The images of Baku and Istanbul were additionally created specifically for this research exercise. Still other pictures were included in my photographic book, *Arabian Transfer*.[6] Some photographs are published in this volume for the first time.

My photographic narrative here begins with several views taken from above, a perspective I knowingly use to introduce the readers to the general urban theme. It then moves progressively toward approaches on the ground, including some at close-range, in and near buildings. In the individual chapters, my images are meant to reveal just how common iconographic elements and design schemes recur across different cities and indeed world regions. In some cases, the projects are real transfers; the developer or the architect have reproduced the same basic design from one city to another. But architectural structures intended as stand-alone icons become – as these photos also make evident – different by what and who is around. Those details and the respective captions help inform the reader of where on earth the shot was made.

Whatever the similarities, contrived or otherwise, each of these cities has its own history and trajectory. Photography can assist, in league with other modes of inquiry, in tracing what has come before and what might be the future unfoldings. As method, conjoined in ways suggested herein, it is worthy of complexities and indeterminacies that the Gulf, perhaps more than other world regions, brings to the fore.

---

[6] Nastasi, M. (2021). *Arabian Transfer.* Berlin: Hatje Cantz.

Abu Dhabi, 2010 (next pages)
View of Al Sowwah Island

Gulf cities – through their extremes –
make visible emerging trends
less noticeable in other world regions.

See the Gulf,
See the World

The newest, fastest, and even the most 'outlandish' of cities have lessons to teach us. Such places can reveal trends less visible in more conventional urban settings. Hardly a mirage emerging out of the desert sands, Gulf cities show much about the global circulation of ideas, investments, designs, technologies, and people. Gulf cities receive, test, alter, and export new ways of making and using urban space. Even when designed and engineered for the Gulf, these new urban arrangements quickly spread internationally.

This book thus investigates Gulf urbanism as it connects to the world. We do not presume the West to be the source of knowledge and initiatives with eventual consequences for the East. Instead, the Gulf allows us to trace actual and potential impacts – as empirical matters – West to East and East to West. Just as in its time the desert city of Las Vegas, parched and on the geographic edge, was famously able to offer lessons about architecture and urbanism more generally, so it is that Gulf cities now can cast new light on the urban world.

Extreme
but not Exceptional

De-exceptionalizing Gulf cities allows for the comparison of places, projects, and processes as they actually exist and also what may occur elsewhere. The immense scale and fast pace construction in the Gulf region magnify aspects typically less evident as urban phenomena. Seeing the Gulf clearly means suspending prejudices temporarily and – to the extent possible – judgment. These are places of subtle complexities, neither mired in a backwards past nor an instance for some version of a returning Arab glory. Whether intended as high-tech utopias or taken to signal impending ecological catastrophe, they do display extreme versions of how contemporary settlements can take shape in astonishing ways.

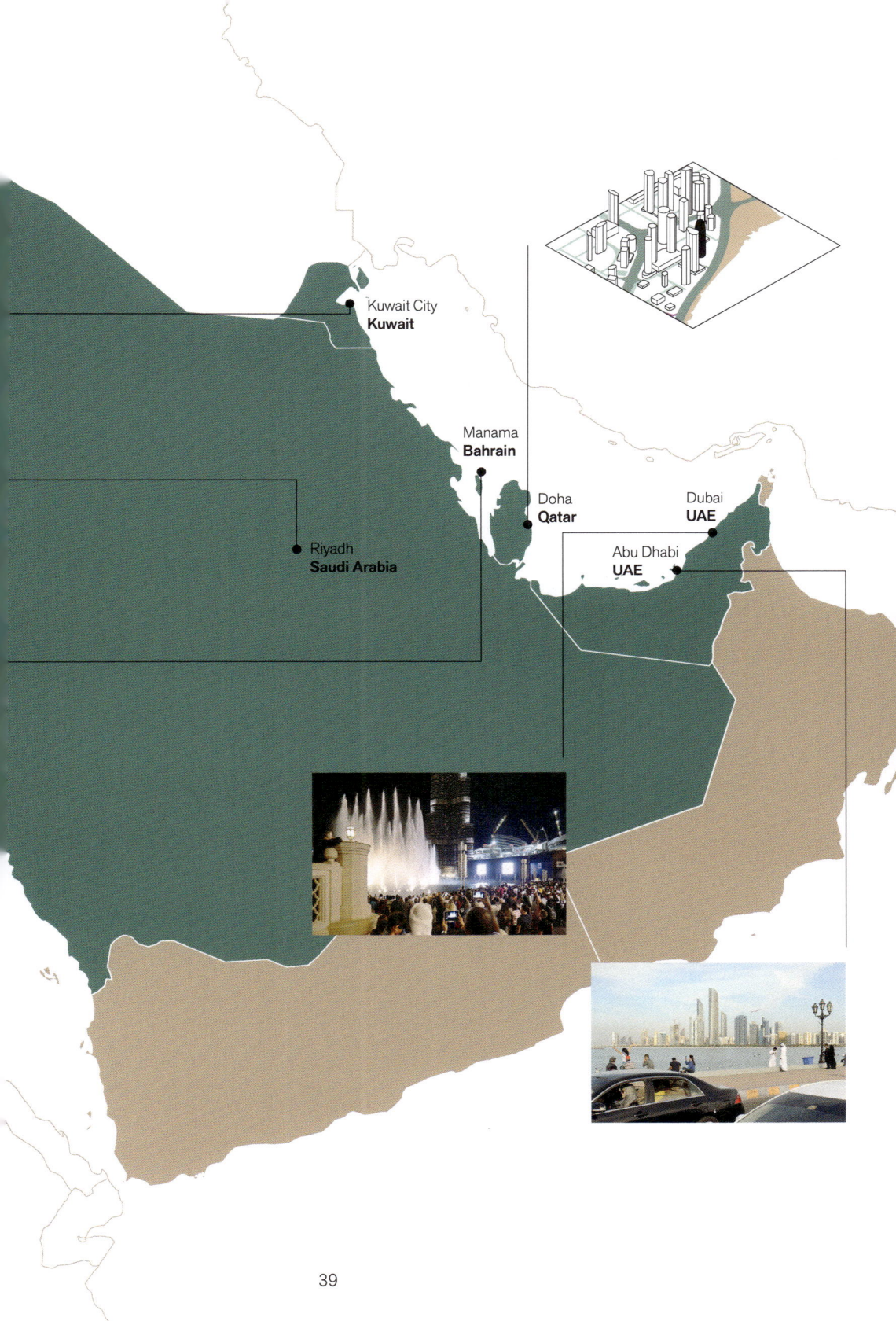

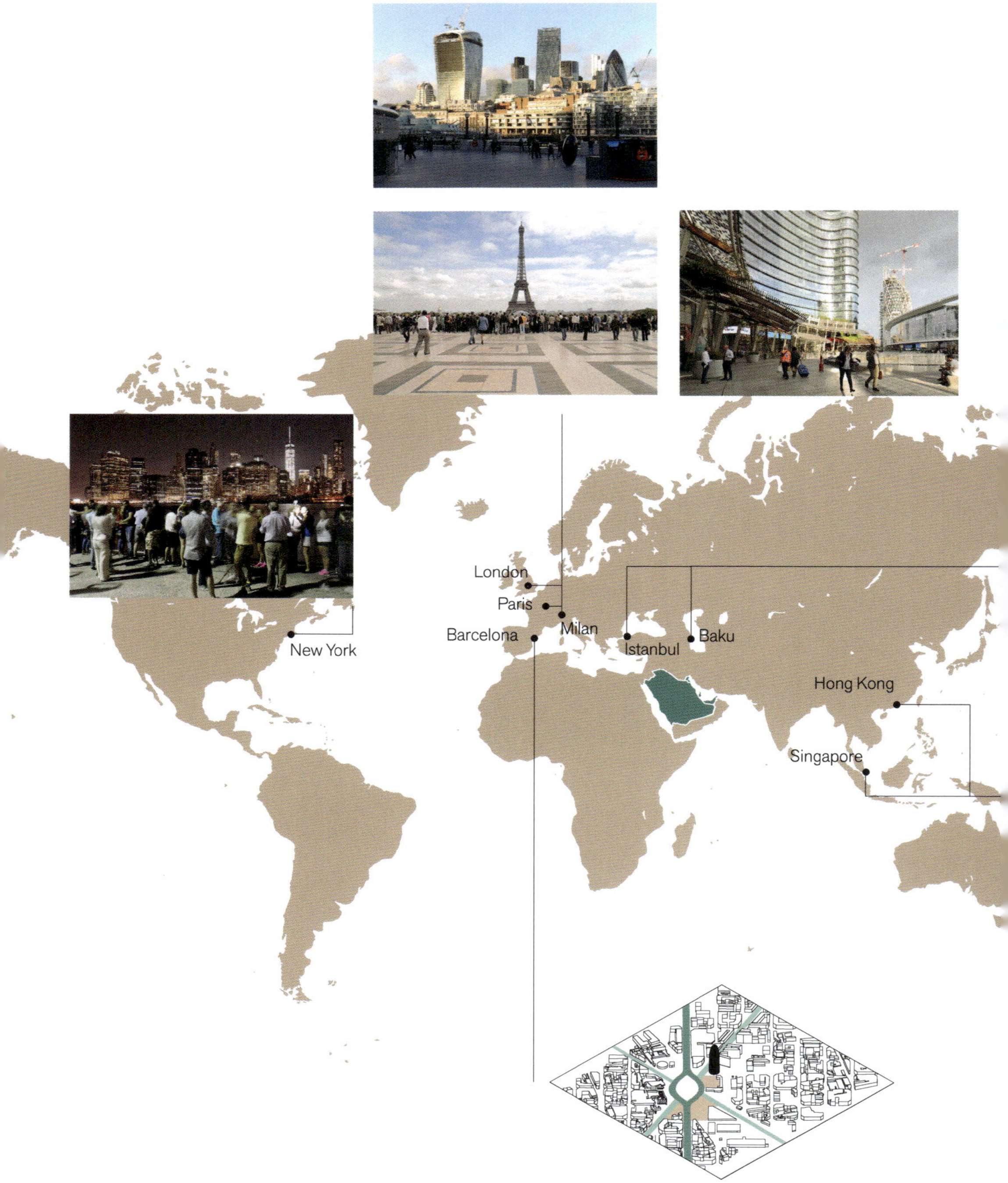
London
Paris
Milan
Barcelona
New York
Istanbul
Baku
Hong Kong
Singapore

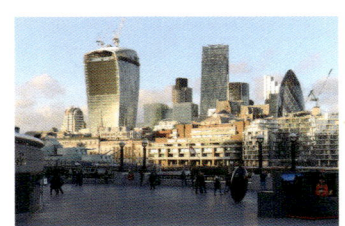

Gulf Cities
of this World

Across the Gulf, there is presence of architects, urban planners, real estate developers, and financiers with a global reach. No longer limited to 'showcase cities' like Dubai, Doha, and Abu Dhabi, the linkages travel to more established urban centers like New York, London, Paris, Barcelona, Hong Kong, and Singapore, often involving many of the same players.

Beyond what meets the eye, we uncover parallel institutional and political arrangements aligning across diverse regions. We illustrate and document these varying urban outcomes, materials, and approaches through photographs, maps, and other graphics. We draw on examples from across the Middle East as well as from the Western and Asian worlds.

Gulf Cities are Connected Transnationally

Whatever actual role it may play in enhancing 'world trade,' Abu Dhabi's 'World Trade Center' (the building pictured below) helped to signify, with its towering height and sleek Norman Foster facade, an impending international prominence. The UAE has become a world leader in creating legal and organizational innovations such as Free Trade Zones and other kinds of special areas for tax-free commerce and relief from financial or religious restrictions. In terms of size, Gulf cities do not figure among the world's largest. However, they have grown fast and they punch above their demographic weight. With access to great wealth, and guided by accomplished foreign experts, transnationalism has become a defining feature – from how land developments take place, to what residents can consume, to who is welcomed in (or kept out).

Gulf city spectacularism, in terms of buildings, airports, and everything else, serves to impress world business and culture.

Riyadh, 2017 (previous pages)
View of King Fahad Road

Abu Dhabi, 2017
View from World Trade Center
Abu Dhabi

Total metropolitan population
(millions, 2018)

Source
UN2014 and UN2018
Revision of World Urbanization Prospects
* 2014 datum

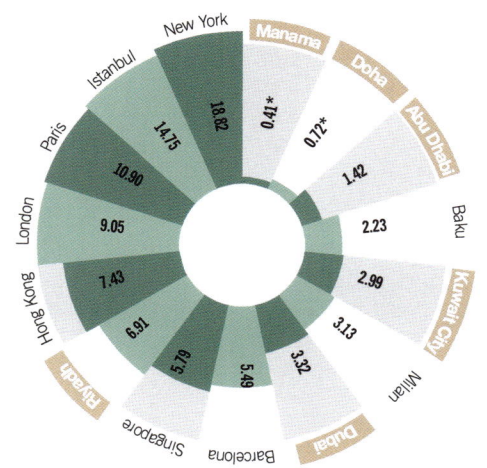

Metropolitan population growth
(percentage, 2000-2015)

Source
UN2014 Revision of World
Urbanization Prospects

City GDP per capita
(thousands US$, 2014)

Source
World Bank and Oxford Brookings
*National

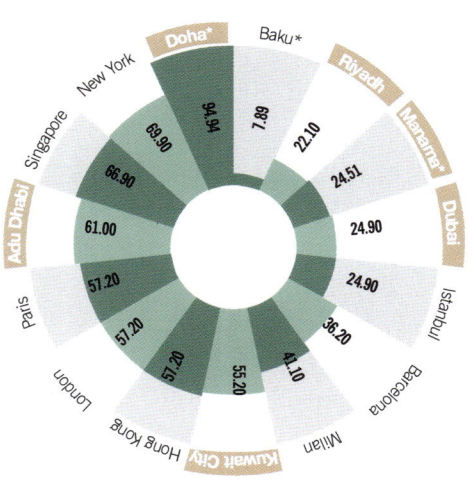

'Business friendly' city ranking

1	2	3	4	12	26	27	42	45	57	91
New York	London	Hong Kong	Singapore	Dubai	Abu Dhabi	Paris	Doha	Milan	Kuwait City	Riyadh

Ranking above is based on quality of business environment, financial sector development, infrastructure, human capital, and 'reputation' of each city. Source Z/Yen Group, 2019 Global Financial Index

Top 15 sovereign wealth funds by assets (billions US$)

Country	Fund	Assets	
Norway	Government Pension Fund - Global	885	$$$$$$$$$$
China	China Investment Corporation	813.8	$$$$$$$$$
UAE	Abu Dhabi Investment Authority	792	$$$$$$$$
Kuwait	Kuwait Investment Authority	592	$$$$$$$
Saudi Arabia	SAMA Foreign Holdings	576.3	$$$$$$
China	SAFE Investment Company	474	$$$$$
China - Hong Kong	Hong Kong Monetary Authority Investment Portfolio	456.6	$$$$$
Singapore	Government of Singapore Investment Corporation	350	$$$$$
Qatar	Qatar Investment Authority	335	$$$$$
China	National Society Security Fund	295	$$$$$
UAE	Investment Corporation of Dubai	200.5	$$$$
Singapore	Temasek Holdings	180	$$$
Saudi Arabia	Public Investment Fund	160	$$$
UAE	Mubadala Investment Company	125	$$$
UAE	Abu Dhabi Investment Council	110	$$$

Source Sovereign Wealth Fund Institute, 2017

Business Eager, Inequality Accepting

Despite overall weakness in human capital and mixed reputation of governance structures, Dubai, Abu Dhabi, and Doha do well in 'Business Friendliness' – higher than, for example, Italy's main economic center, Milan. Wage and labor structures, along with legal arrangements, incentivize international investment and trade. With access to their enormously resourced sovereign wealth funds – among the largest in the world – investment routinely flows toward international ventures along with funding domestic initiatives. Giant revenues for the privileged exist alongside the severe deprivation of the many. Official citizens share in the affluence that makes the ruling families so extraordinarily rich. It is the migrant workers at the bottom who live in hardship. Radical inequality is unapologetically acknowledged and clearly visible – labor camps are massive and conditions at work sites can be harsh.

Dubai, 2017
Sheikh Zayed Road

The Force of Migration

Of all countries globally, the UAE ranks first in proportion of population made up by migrants – at 88%. Qatar is second with 79%, and Kuwait third with 72%. In Western countries, the national/foreign ratio is typically reversed: France, for example, is comprised of 87% nationals and only 13% immigrants. Gulf cities rely heavily on migrants for construction, but also for routine services like catering, road maintenance, and domestic labor. Foreigners also perform the bulk of professional and management tasks. In exchange for their efforts, they are paid much higher wages than would be possible in their home countries.

The top five sending countries to the UAE are – in order of magnitude – India, Bangladesh, Pakistan, Egypt, and the Philippines. In part because of proximity and long-established routes of travel and trade, South Asia is the primary source. There is also a tilt toward English-speakers – important for taxi driving, other tourist services, and employment as domestics with nannies and care-givers typically coming from the Philippines. Except for those at higher rungs (like professionals), marriage and family unification are not a valid basis for residence. Overall, recruitment is heavily for single men.

Dubai, 2012
Al Satwa Neighborhood

Kuwait City, 2017 (next pages)
Jaber Al-Mubarak Street

Immigrant populations
(percents and numbers)

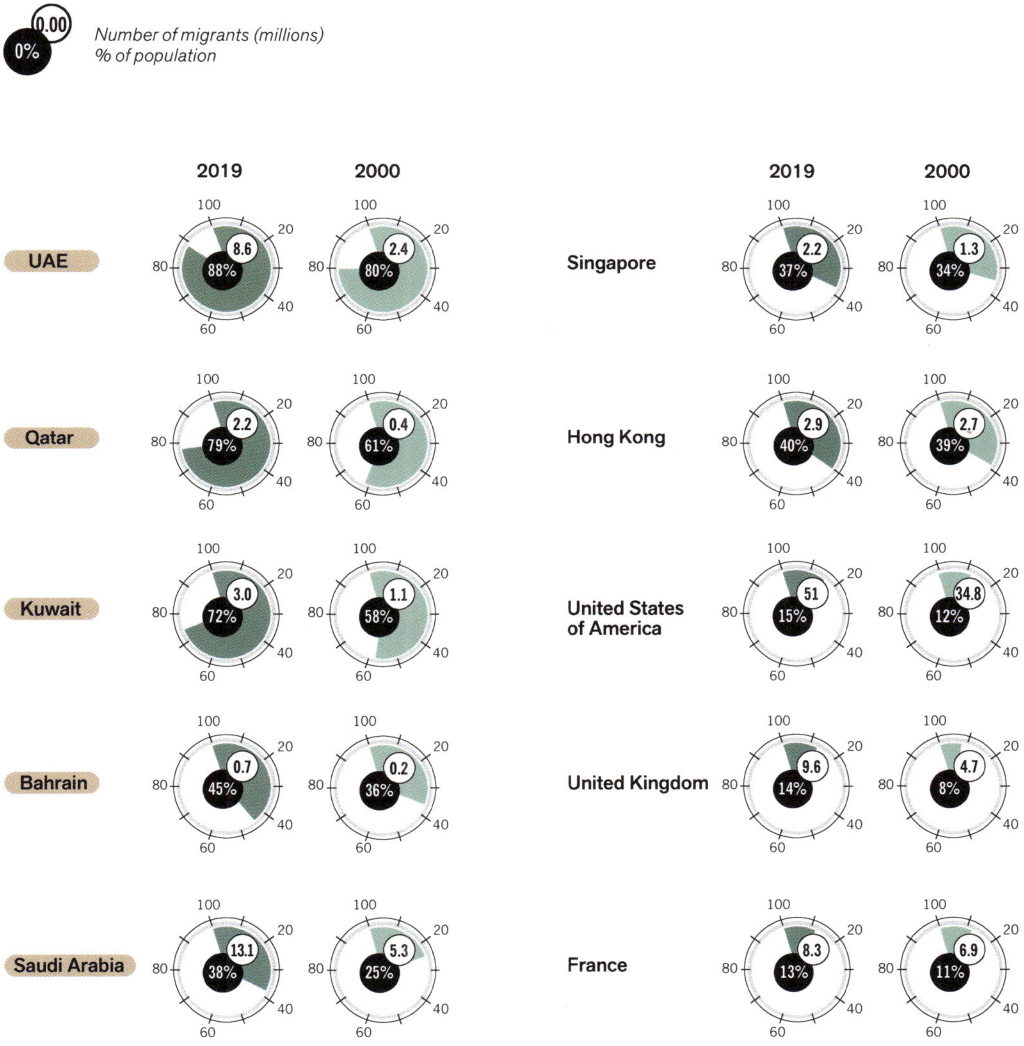

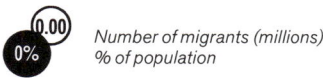
Number of migrants (millions)
% of population

	2019	2000		2019	2000
UAE	8.6 / 88%	2.4 / 80%	**Singapore**	2.2 / 37%	1.3 / 34%
Qatar	2.2 / 79%	0.4 / 61%	**Hong Kong**	2.9 / 40%	2.7 / 39%
Kuwait	3.0 / 72%	1.1 / 58%	**United States of America**	51 / 15%	34.8 / 12%
Bahrain	0.7 / 45%	0.2 / 36%	**United Kingdom**	9.6 / 14%	4.7 / 8%
Saudi Arabia	13.1 / 38%	5.3 / 25%	**France**	8.3 / 13%	6.9 / 11%

Source
UN DESA International
Migrant Stock 2019 data

Individual Trajectories

Gulf citizens are born with access to government-provided health care, education, and comfortable housing. Jobs also come from the government; in the Qatari case, the public sector employs 80% of labor-active citizens, according to recent estimates. Even when working in the private sphere, including foreign businesses, government rules mandate higher salaries for citizens than their (well-paid) colleagues from other countries. High wages are complemented with other job-related benefits including cars, drivers, and personal assistants. Migrants maintain only weak legal rights and have virtually no chance of becoming citizens. Their

Abu Dhabi, 2010
Street Crossing near the National Bank of Abu Dhabi

work contracts are of limited duration and not necessarily guaranteed to be renewed. Severe as conditions can be, Gulf cities evidently provide opportunities not otherwise readily available. They facilitate long-distance remittances for children's education, family medical care, housing, and other quality of life benefits.

Riyadh, 2017
Riyadh Street Portrait

Spectacularizing the urban environment
attracts investment and tourists.
Other types of urban goals are less
evidently fulfilled.

City Icons
for the World

The architectural race to the top has become a modern game for many cities. Looking at recent trends, we can trace the trajectory of the title of world's tallest building as starting in Europe then passing to North America, followed by Asia, and landing recently in the Gulf.

For the last two decades, the geography of world's tallest building has clearly shifted, with Gulf cities in the lead. As of 2020, Gulf cities retain the world's tallest as well as third tallest building while the One World Trade Center in New York is the only building from any Western city making an appearance in the top ten.

Even when similar in height or girth, surrounding particularities of cityscape change how the icon building operates as part of life and economy. In this chapter, we compare the Eiffel Tower in Paris to the Burj Khalifa in Dubai. True to form, icons are often meant to bolster national stature, more so than respond to commercial land-use pressure or to public betterment goals. In the Gulf, this goes to the extreme.

Urban Icons

The Eiffel Tower was once ridiculed by Parisians as a 'stupefying folly.' Today this engineering marvel, for a time the tallest structure on earth, serves as an internationally recognized symbol for both the city and the nation – it also attracts more paying visitors than any monument anywhere. If the Eiffel Tower marked Paris as a center of modernity, the spectacular Burj Khalifa symbolizes Dubai as its hypermodern successor. It is replete with musically choreographed fountains – also the world's largest. As with the Eiffel before it, the Burj represents a spectacular building capable of shifting a territory's image within the global collective imagination.

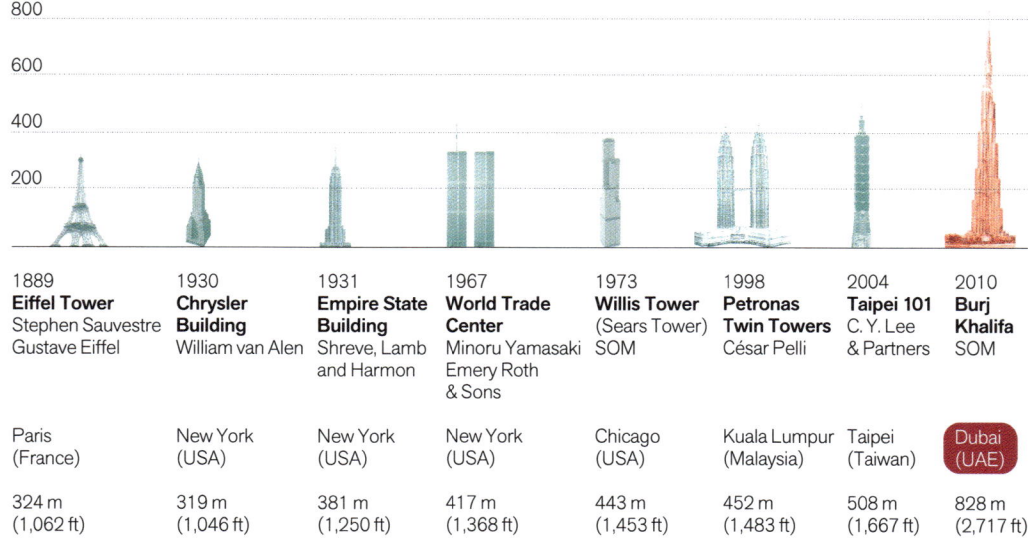

Timeline of the tallest building in the world and their designers after the Eiffel Tower

Source
Council on Tall Buildings and Urban Habitat – Skyscraper Center
(existing buildings - December 31, 2016)

1889	1930	1931	1967	1973	1998	2004	2010
Eiffel Tower	**Chrysler Building**	**Empire State Building**	**World Trade Center**	**Willis Tower** (Sears Tower)	**Petronas Twin Towers**	**Taipei 101**	**Burj Khalifa**
Stephen Sauvestre Gustave Eiffel	William van Alen	Shreve, Lamb and Harmon	Minoru Yamasaki Emery Roth & Sons	SOM	César Pelli	C. Y. Lee & Partners	SOM
Paris (France)	New York (USA)	New York (USA)	New York (USA)	Chicago (USA)	Kuala Lumpur (Malaysia)	Taipei (Taiwan)	Dubai (UAE)
324 m (1,062 ft)	319 m (1,046 ft)	381 m (1,250 ft)	417 m (1,368 ft)	443 m (1,453 ft)	452 m (1,483 ft)	508 m (1,667 ft)	828 m (2,717 ft)

Dubai, 2010
Downtown Dubai and Burj Khalifa

Paris, 2010
Eiffel Tower Seen from Montparnasse Tower

Dubai, 2017 (next pages)
View from Burj Khalifa Observation Deck

Spectacular Competitions, from the Ground Up

Reflecting landscape ideals from its time, the Eiffel Tower stands amidst formal gardens with rectilinear paths and edges. Beyond serving as just a focal point for grand views, it also sustains, as a way-finding reference, city life and activities at a smaller, more immediate scale.

The surrounding city fabric provides distinct populations with open-ended uses of public space and pedestrian links to other parts of the city.

In contrast, the Burj Khalifa relies on technology and retail to define the urban experience. The adjacent Dubai Mall is the largest shopping center in the world. Beyond the Burj, other Gulf structures, theme parks, and Grand Prix raceways also break records. More so than for many other world attractions, Gulf city spectacles' identity and meaning are grounded in bigness and extravaganza as opposed to creating contexts that promote activities at a human scale.

2020's top ten tallest buildings in the world

*Source
Council on Tall Buildings and Urban Habitat – Skyscraper Center
(existing buildings – December 31, 2020)*

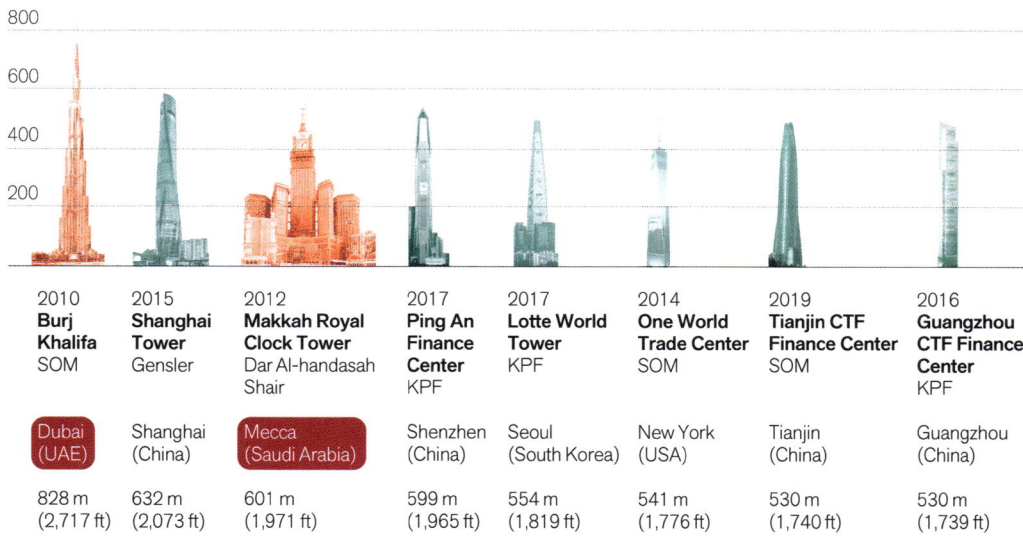

2010	2015	2012	2017	2017	2014	2019	2016
Burj Khalifa	**Shanghai Tower**	**Makkah Royal Clock Tower**	**Ping An Finance Center**	**Lotte World Tower**	**One World Trade Center**	**Tianjin CTF Finance Center**	**Guangzhou CTF Finance Center**
SOM	Gensler	Dar Al-handasah Shair	KPF	KPF	SOM	SOM	KPF
Dubai (UAE)	Shanghai (China)	Mecca (Saudi Arabia)	Shenzhen (China)	Seoul (South Korea)	New York (USA)	Tianjin (China)	Guangzhou (China)
828 m (2,717 ft)	632 m (2,073 ft)	601 m (1,971 ft)	599 m (1,965 ft)	554 m (1,819 ft)	541 m (1,776 ft)	530 m (1,740 ft)	530 m (1,739 ft)

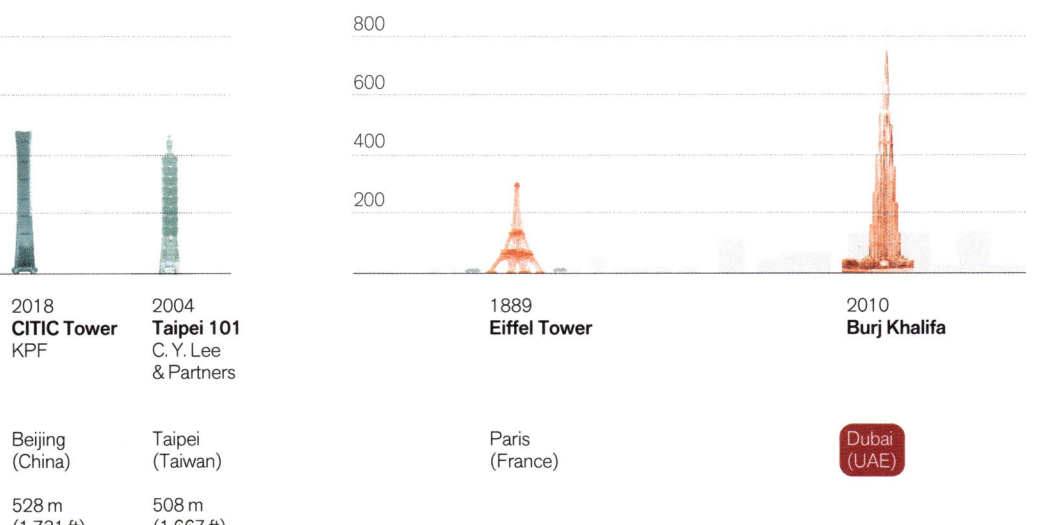

2018	2004	1889	2010
CITIC Tower	**Taipei 101**	**Eiffel Tower**	**Burj Khalifa**
KPF	C. Y. Lee & Partners		
Beijing (China)	Taipei (Taiwan)	Paris (France)	Dubai (UAE)
528 m (1,731 ft)	508 m (1,667 ft)		

Dubai, 2015 (next pages)
View from Al Satwa

Icons on the Land

In utilizing outdoor spaces, Gulf cities are challenged by unbearable heat and humidity for much of the year. In cities like New York, a more temperate climate combines with long-standing civic ideologies to create a contrasting and more varied urbanism. While still monumental and large in scale, public spaces have been deliberately set aside for recreation and to foster interaction across a wide range of social classes. Visually, and as a matter of human experience, cities like New York, and still older ones like London and Paris, present an urban environment filled with buildings mixed in terms of age, height, materials, and style.

The skylines of New York and Dubai are both spectacular, but they take on vastly different meanings when experienced directly. Gulf city public spaces tend to be more limited in their ambition and outcomes. Abu Dhabi, Dubai, and Doha (as well as other cities in the Gulf) are generally not well-provisioned with parks. Most notable are their seaside 'corniches'

which, despite providing ample landscaping, lack easy access. The vast majority of residents are excluded by either logistics or regulations. Medium and low-income migrant workers instead find leftover precincts like roadside shoulders, interior blocks, or vacant parcels awaiting real estate development to meet and pass free time – as can be seen on the previous pages showing men playing cricket. Transition and impermanence are everywhere and are on prominent display.

New York, 2009
View from Sheep Meadow, Central Park

Dubai has more international overnight visitors than New York. Already challenging other world capitals, Dubai's visitor numbers and spending continue to climb.

Tourist City as Hub

Rather than deriving from natural wonders, holy sites, or historic venues, tourism in cities like Abu Dhabi, Doha and Dubai is a designed-in feature. Intrinsic to the strategy are gigantic-scale airports, top-level national airlines, iconic attractions, hotels of conspicuous luxury, and world-class shopping.

In this manner, Gulf cities have climbed their way up as places for recreation, doing business, or as convenient stopover – in effect becoming city-scale prototypes of world tourism hubs. With massive infrastructure investments, these new global cities are thus purpose-built into existence, rather than depending on gradual historic evolution or vagaries of changing traveler preference.

Dubai as a Tourism Hub

The strategy of staging the city, with varying degrees of deliberateness, spreads around the world. New York has the 'founding' skyline, albeit one that was an after-effect of various building booms. Far afield, Hong Kong (see page 75) shows itself off with a 'Symphony of Lights,' performed nightly by its skyline. Gulf cities follow these precedents, helping them reach ever higher numbers of tourist visitors. Dubai has more international overnight visitors than New York and is ranked just behind London and Paris. In recent years, Dubai has been among the most successful cities in the world in growing overnight international stays. It ranks highest in per capita spending of overnight visitors. In part this results from serving as a stopover for travel to other business or pleasure destinations but also from Dubai itself becoming a tourist destination.

Dubai, 2015 (previous pages)
Dubai Fountain
and Burj Khalifa

New York, 2015
Lower Manhattan
Seen from Pier 1, Brooklyn

International overnight visitors (millions)

Source
Our own calculations based on Global Destination Cities Index report

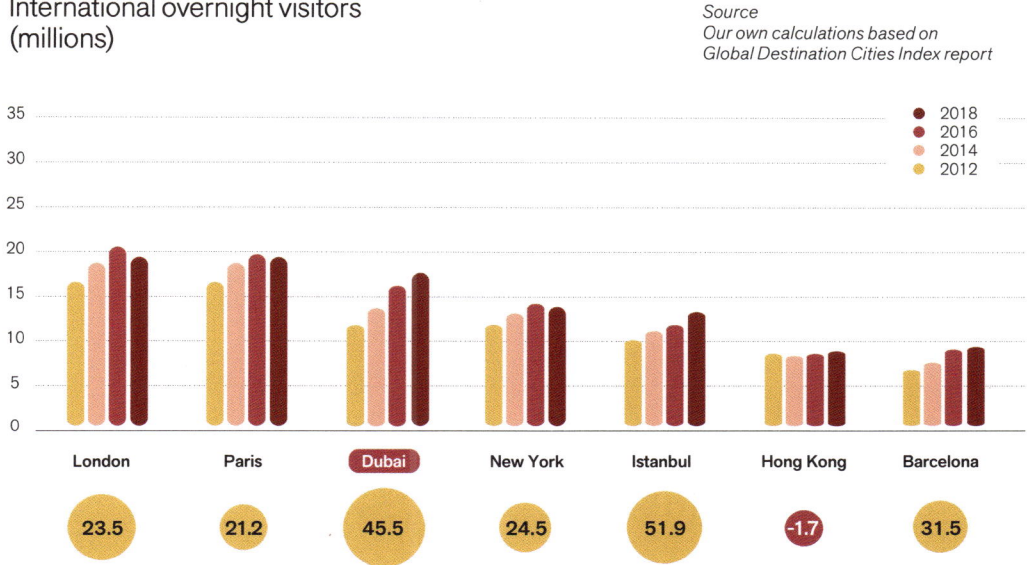

Rate of increase (%), 2012-2018

Aggregate visitor spending (billions US$)

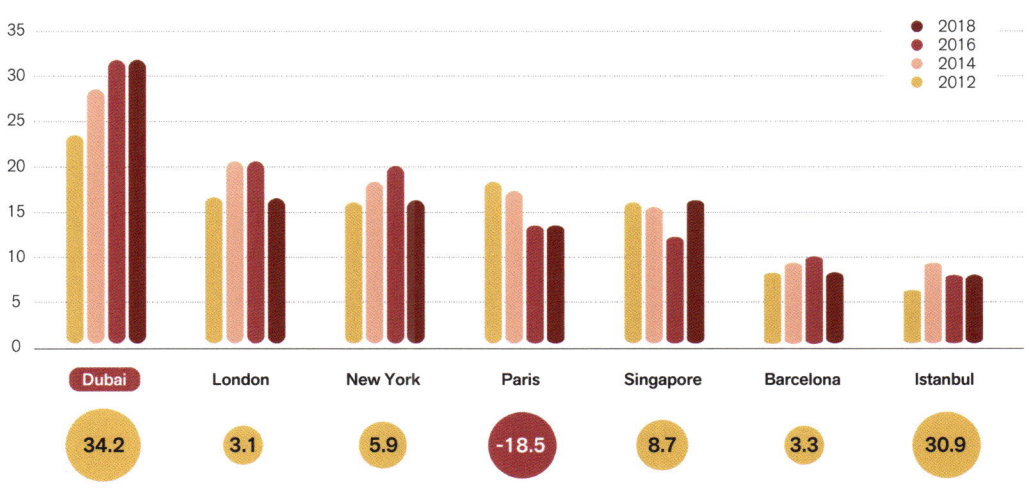

Rate of increase (%), 2012-2018

Race for Passengers

Gulf airport passenger numbers are sharply on the rise. Gulf-based airlines occupy the top spots in world-class quality, based on passenger evaluations.
The high-ranking of airlines helps brand the region's other services and offerings as similarly excellent, bolstering demand for the region's luxury hotels, restaurants, and tourist attractions.

Heights, size, and glamor — of record-breaking buildings, fountains, and malls — similarly signal attainments available for purchase — as real estate, jewelry or, increasingly, art from local galleries. The culture industries grow, along with greater capacities for logistics and commercial transaction.

Top 10 airports by passenger numbers (millions)

2007

Rank	Airport	Passengers
1	Atlanta - ATL	89.4
2	Chicago - ORD	76.9
3	London - LHR	68.1
4	Tokyo - HND	66.8
5	Los Angeles - LAX	61.9
6	Paris - CDG	59.9
7	Dallas - DFW	59.8
8	Frankfurt - FRA	54.2
9	Beijing - PEK	53.6
10	Madrid - MAD	52.1
13	New York - JFK	47.7
14	Hong Kong - HKG	47.0
19	Singapore - SIN	36.7
27	**Dubai - DXB**	**34.3**

2015

Rank	Passengers	Airport
1	101.5	Atlanta - ATL
2	89.9	Beijing - PEK
3	**78.0**	**Dubai - DXB**
4	76.9	Chicago - ORD
5	75.3	Tokyo - HND
6	75.0	London - LHR
7	74.9	Los Angeles - LAX
8	68.3	Hong Kong - HKG
9	65.8	Paris - CDG
10	64.1	Dallas - DFW
11	61.8	Istanbul - IST
15	56.8	New York - JFK
16	55.4	Singapore - SIN

Source
Airports Council International

2016's top 10 airlines
by quality evaluation

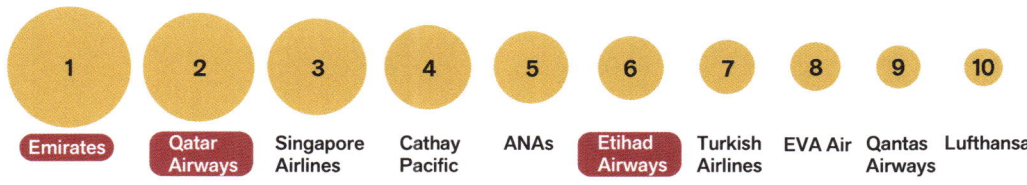

1	2	3	4	5	6	7	8	9	10
Emirates	Qatar Airways	Singapore Airlines	Cathay Pacific	ANAs	Etihad Airways	Turkish Airlines	EVA Air	Qantas Airways	Lufthansa

Source
The World Airline Award

Hong Kong, 2013
Hong Kong from Tsim Sha Tsui

Dubai, 2017 (next pages)
Canal Khor

Replicating building types that have succeeded in one place reassures investors – distant or local – while also lowering design costs. The original project gets modified as it travels, with context changing its urban qualities.

Buildings Travel

Even when designed by the same firm according to a similar type, buildings change as they travel from one city to another. One factor is thus the need (or not) to defer to local residents and authorities. 'Gulf cities' architectural exuberance is in part due to fast-track governance along with readily available capital, low-cost labor, and 'friendly' business climates which facilitate the experiments that can then be transferred to other cities around the world.

Gulf cities function as a sort of 'urban testbed' for projects that may travel, in an adjusted form, to other international locations. The iterations sent out from the Gulf may be even larger in size and constructed at even greater speeds after learning from the original experience.

Three projects by the UK-based Broadway Malyan show how complex plans adjust themselves to the urban context where they land – in this case Abu Dhabi (UAE), London (UK), and Baku (Azerbaijan).

Far-Flung Locations of Projects Designed by Broadway Malyan

The UK-based multinational design firm Broadway Malyan has completed six projects in the UAE since 2011. With 16 offices and hundreds of employees, it is active across Europe and Asia. The impact of the Broadway Malyan project on the desert shoreline of Abu Dhabi significantly contrasts the similar scheme, by the same firm, when placed in London's post-industrial Battersea Reach area – changing still again with installation at Port Baku, Azerbaijan.

London
Battersea Reach

Broadway Maylan
completed projects 1998-2019

● Project location
○ Location of projects selected for comparison

Sources
based on Ponzini, D. (2020). *Transnational Architecture and Urbanism: Rethinking How Cities Plan, Transform, and Learn.* London: Routledge, p. 184;
www.broadwaymalyan.com

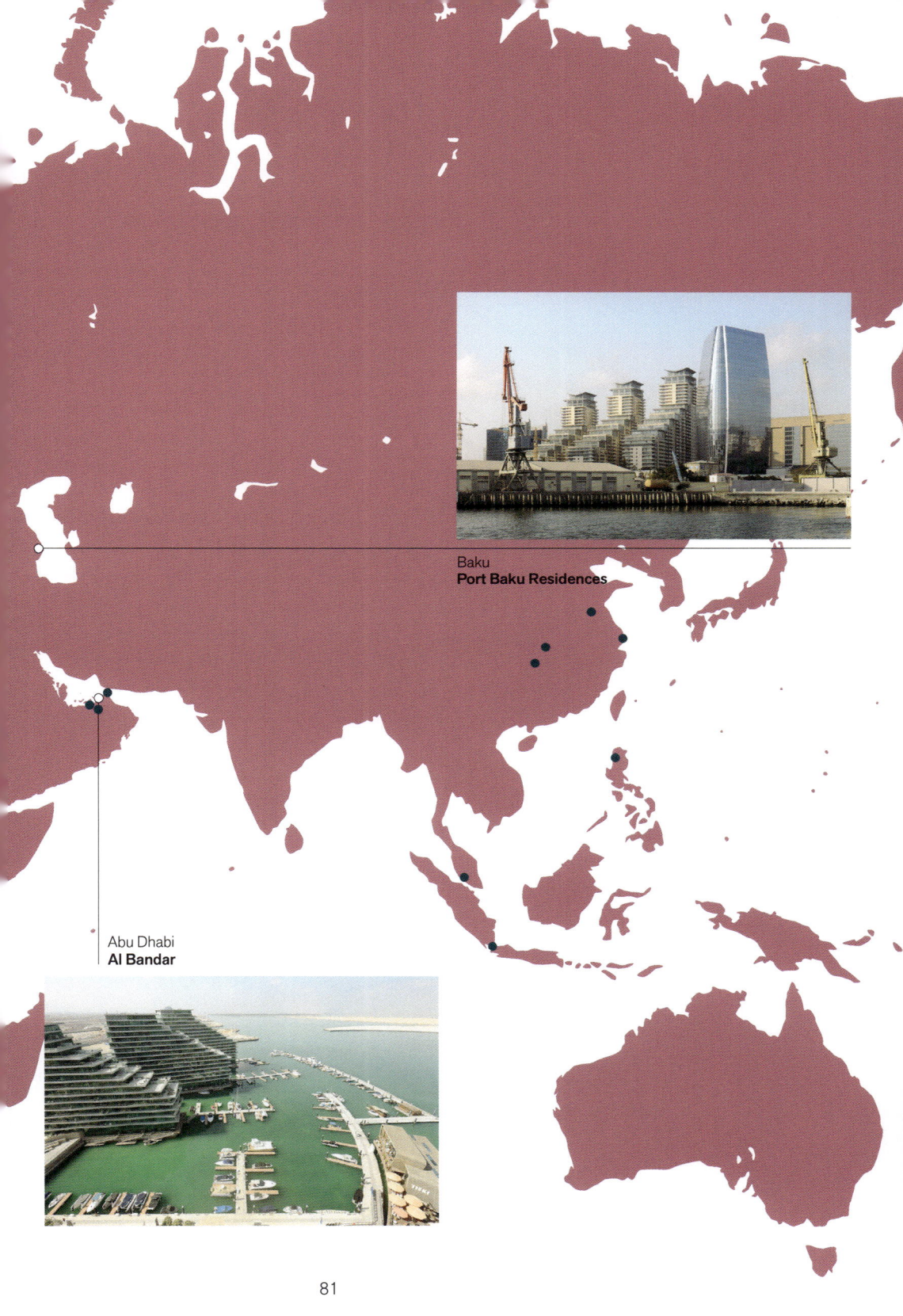

Baku
Port Baku Residences

Abu Dhabi
Al Bandar

Similar Forms, Different Landing

Broadway Malyan's projects landed differently in Abu Dhabi, London, and Baku. The three barge-like buildings for the waterfront of Abu Dhabi took four years to build. Their counterpart project in London (at Battersea Reach), although smallest in scale, took 11 years. Together with London's St. George Wharf development, by the same firm, they inspired a similar, yet even larger project for Baku in Azerbaijan.

This final iteration required only five years to be completed. Impediments and opportunities occur for technical reasons, by scale of project, and also from local political and citizenry involvement. The London project (i.e. the smallest version) started first and required the largest amount of time to complete.

Abu Dhabi, 2010 (previous pages) Abu Dhabi, 2017
Al Bandar   Al Bandar

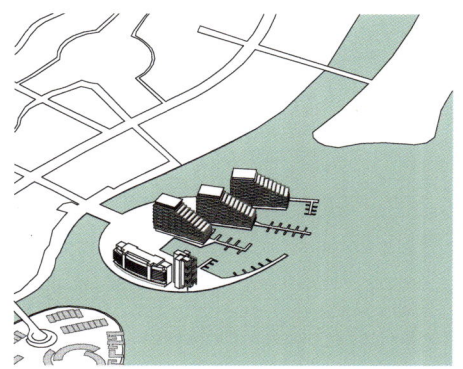

Abu Dhabi (UAE)
Al Bandar

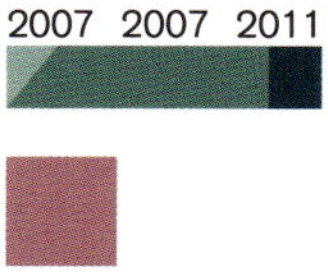

2007 2007 2011

Total surface:
90,000 sqm (968,750 sq ft)

Project phases and building size
- Appointment
- Construction
- Completion
- Total surface

Abu Dhabi, 2015
Al Bandar

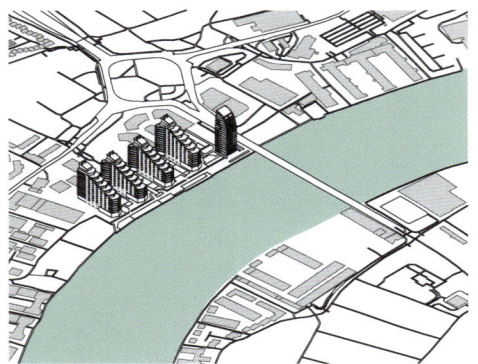

**London (UK)
Battersea Residences**

2000　　2004　　　　　　　2011

Total surface:
31,000 sqm (333,680 sq ft)

Project phases and building size
- Appointment
- Construction
- Completion
- Total surface

London, 2015
Battersea Reach

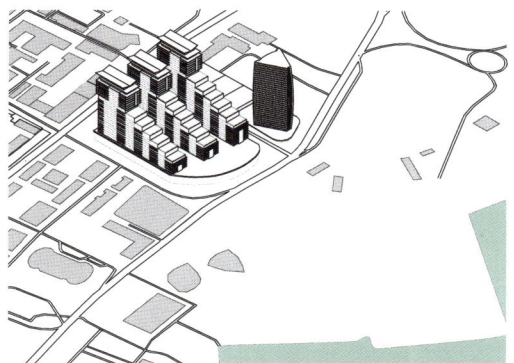

**Baku (Azerbaijan)
Port Baku Residences**

2009 2010   2014

Total surface:
400,000 sqm (4,305,560 sq ft)

Project phases and building size

- Appointment
- Construction
- Completion
- Total surface

Baku, 2017
Port Baku Residences

Manama, 2017 (next pages)
View from Al Ghous

The quality of an urban space does not simply derive from building design. Contextual features inevitably shape urban impact and meaning.

Landmarks Can't Travel

Trying to import branded landmarks into a foreign location seldom works. The way people experience the urban realm and view its landmarks, both from near and afar, does not depend solely on the virtuosity of transnational designers. Shifts in context alter impact and undermine the meaning of any building, even more so of iconic architectural pieces. Such design mobility – not only to and around the Gulf, but also from the Gulf to other places – shows the limits of attempts to borrow or reproduce specific features of architectural icons.

Two projects by French architect Jean Nouvel in Barcelona and Doha illustrate how iconic architecture lands contrastingly in different urban contexts.

Locations of Architect Jean Nouvel's Projects

Paris-based Jean Nouvel leads a transnational design firm with dozens of completed projects in over 25 countries. Two of his most iconic endeavors have been inaugurated recently in the Gulf: the Louvre Abu Dhabi (2017) and the National Museum in Doha (2019). Here we compare two of his prior works: an iconic tower in Barcelona and its 'match' in Doha.

Ateliers Jean Nouvel
completed projects 1990-2020

● Project locations
○ Location of projects selected for comparison

Barcelona
Agbar Tower

Doha
Doha Tower

Sources
based on Ponzini, D. (2020). *Transnational Architecture and Urbanism: Rethinking How Cities Plan, Transform, and Learn.* London: Routledge, p. 232; www.jeannouvel.com and others

Same Architect, Different Contexts

Jean Nouvel's Doha Tower strongly resembles, in terms of form, his earlier work in Barcelona, the Agbar Tower. However, the two towers' radically different contexts generate contrasting experiences, especially when approached at ground level. The Barcelona landmark sits within a close-knit and medium-rise fabric of busy streets and sidewalks. In the car-dependent environment of Doha, buildings exist as independent objects, simply standing aside one another with no direct connections.

The visibility and contribution of the two landmarks to the urban experience respond more to place than architectural aesthetics. On paper and as models, both Barcelona's and Doha's skylines include one iconic building by the star architect Jean Nouvel. But in Barcelona the surrounding medium-rise landscape makes the landmark clearly visible, while in Doha none of the individual pieces of architecture end up as recognizable.

Barcelona, 2011
Agbar Tower from the Sagrada Familia

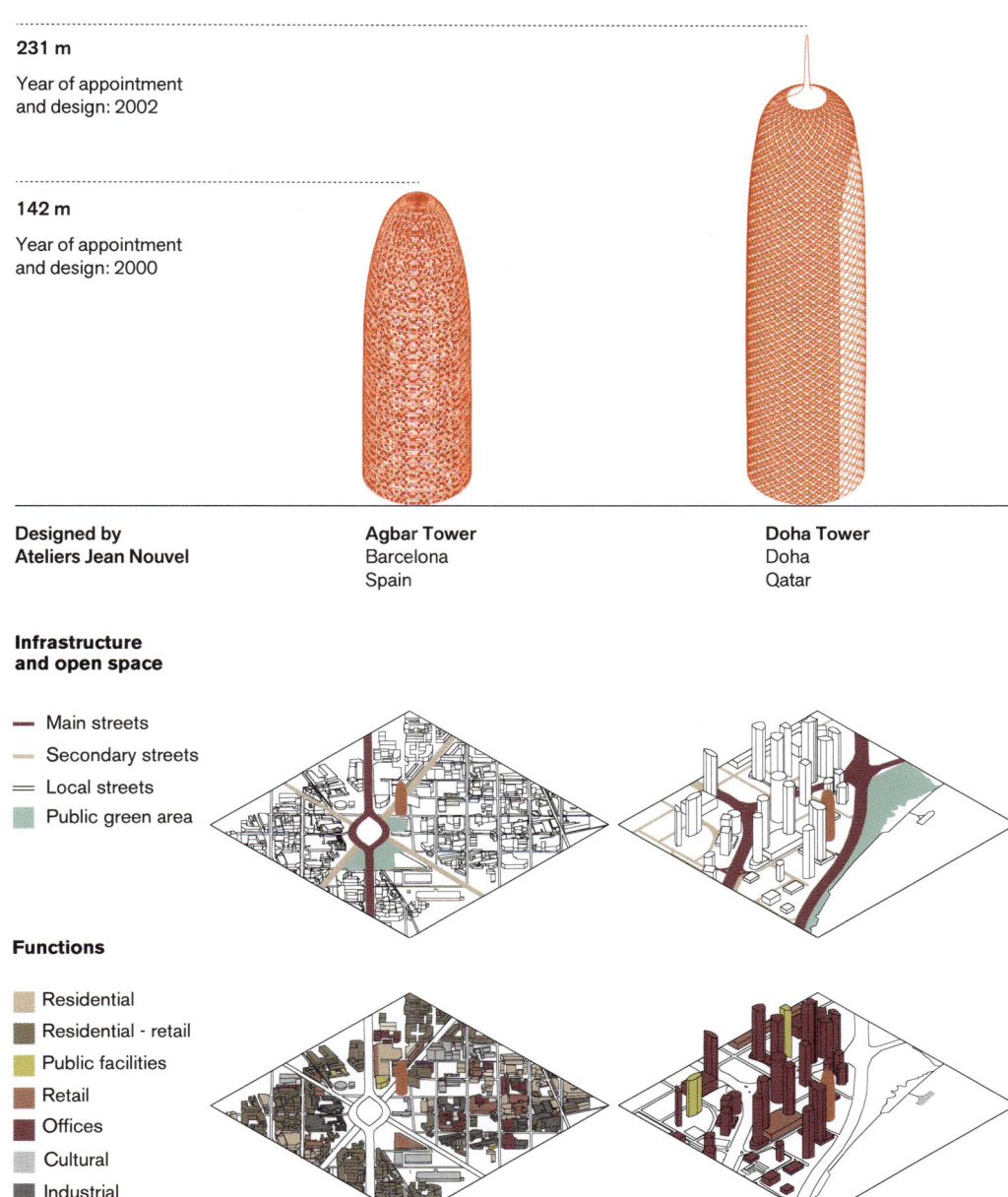

231 m

Year of appointment
and design: 2002

142 m

Year of appointment
and design: 2000

Designed by
Ateliers Jean Nouvel

Agbar Tower
Barcelona
Spain

Doha Tower
Doha
Qatar

Infrastructure
and open space

- Main streets
- Secondary streets
- Local streets
- Public green area

Functions

- Residential
- Residential - retail
- Public facilities
- Retail
- Offices
- Cultural
- Industrial

Sources
Ponzini, D., & Arosio, P. M. (2017). 'Urban effects
of the transnational circulation of branded buildings:
Comparing two skyscrapers and their context in Barcelona
and Doha.' *Urban Design International*, 22(1), 28-46

**Visible Icon
or Tower in a Crowd**

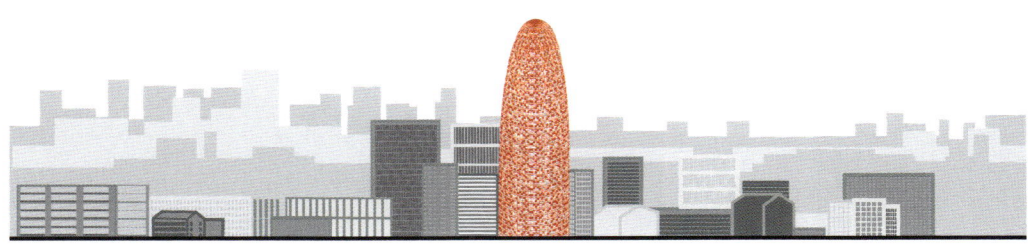

Barcelona, 2011
Glòries and Agbar Tower

Doha, 2017
West Bay with Doha Tower and Others

The Place for Landmarks

Singapore's Marina Bay Sands project and Abu Dhabi's Gate Towers bear a striking visual resemblance but, in this case, were designed by different firms. The Abu Dhabi buildings consist primarily of high-end apartments while its Singaporean counterpart mixes in cultural and recreational functions.

The Singapore hotel complex is topped by a vast swimming pool and accompanied by a popular public park located near its base. Such features have helped turn the complex into a meaningful landmark – not only for the immediate area, but the city as a whole impacting how local residents and visitors apprehend this place.

Doha, 2013 (previous pages)
Realize

Singapore, 2013
Marina Bay Sands

Abu Dhabi, 2015
The Gate Tower

Riyadh, 2017
King Fahd Road and Al Majdoul Tower

A Drill (Bit) in the Urban and Regional Landscape

Spectacular technological advance not only gives architecture a new twist, it also attracts the attention of financers, developers, and visitors. The ambition to create a unique landmark inevitably must come to terms with the surrounding landscape, as well as competition in the region. The twist of the structure and architectural aesthetics of the Al Majdoul Tower in Riyadh indeed differs from that of the United Tower in Bahrain Bay (both in these pages), Manama – as well as from the Cayan Tower in Dubai (following pages), the Al Bidda Tower in Doha, (see page 98) the Al Tijaria Tower in Kuwait City (see page 144), and others in the Gulf region and beyond. However, though each aimed to gain attention for being spectacular, the degree of novelty reduces with each iteration utilizing similar design gimmick.

Manama, 2017
Palace Avenue and United Tower

Dubai, 2017 (next pages)
Dubai Marina Skyline
and Cayan Tower

Gulf-based developers test new projects
locally that can then be exported
and adapted to other cities
in the Middle East and beyond.

Testing and Spreading

Fast-track governance, ample finance, and enterprising real-estate firms facilitate Gulf cities' role as urban 'test beds' for architectural, engineering and design experiments. Gulf cities' accomplishment of superlative projects displays capacity to complete both unique and mundane projects.

Their reputation for big urban investments and luxury lifestyle contributes to increasing demand internationally, where local players seek out such antecedents and features. Even if new and spectacular 'tests' end up with short-term losses locally, replication elsewhere can yield higher returns in the international market.

The case of Emaar Square by the Dubai-based real-estate company Emaar Properties shows how Gulf city enterprise can indeed circulate, at least in terms of format and ambition.

Emaar Projects in the World

Dubai-based Emaar Properties is renowned for its 'headlining accomplishment,' the Burj Khalifa. Its 53 projects now spread over four continents. The company's stated strategy is 'to replicate our Dubai business model and practices in international markets.'

In its international projects, Emaar often partners with other funding sources, limiting its own up-front investment to land acquisition and basic infrastructure. The final result abroad tends to be far less spectacular than the original Dubai-based projects.

Istanbul, 2017
Emaar Square

Dubai, 2017 (next pages)
Downtown Dubai

Emaar Properties project locations, (country breakdown)

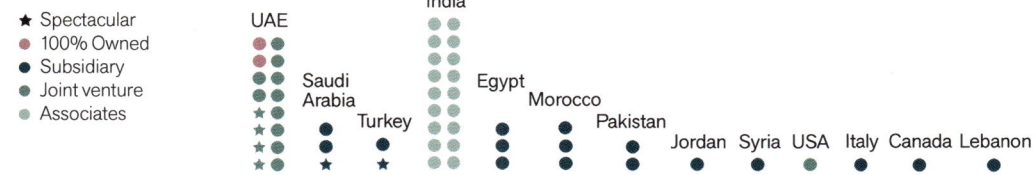

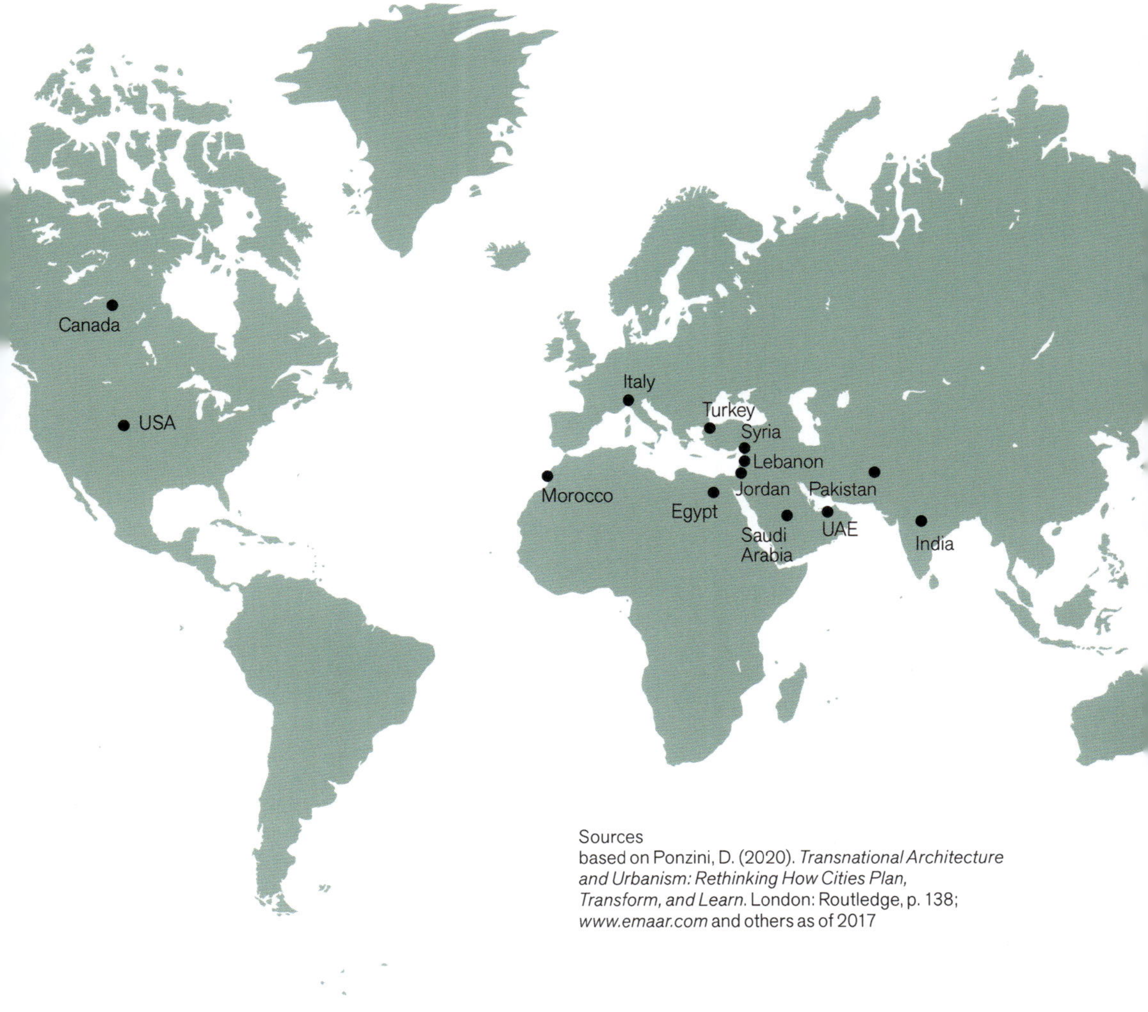

Sources
based on Ponzini, D. (2020). *Transnational Architecture and Urbanism: Rethinking How Cities Plan, Transform, and Learn*. London: Routledge, p. 138; www.emaar.com and others as of 2017

Testing Emaar Squares

Emaar Square in Dubai was completed in the late 2000's, adjacent to the spectacular Burj Khalifa. Although appearing under the same title, the Istanbul version is not a straightforward copy. As with other repeats of Emaar Square branding in the world, local agents attempt to leverage the idea of Gulf luxury and lifestyle without necessarily delivering its substance.

Dubai, 2017
Emaar Square from Burj Khalifa

Istanbul, 2017
Emaar Square

Spreading Emaar Squares in the Middle East

After Dubai's Emaar Square and another Emaar Square completed in Istanbul, additional Emaar Squares are underway in Cairo and Jeddah. While sharing some overall characteristics of scale and mixed-use master-planned communities, they adjust to local specifics of design context, investor interests, and governance arrangements.

Istanbul, 2017
Looking towards Emaar Square

Istanbul
Emaar Square
Completed

Dubai
Emaar Square
Completed

Cairo
Emaar Square
Under constrution

Jeddah
Emaar Square
Under constrution

Source
www.emaar.com

Gulf-based investors shop
for buildings and sites
all over the world, with a noticeable
taste for 'trophy' properties.

Collecting Trophy Buildings

As with investors in general, Gulf real estate investors do not simply 'go global.' They are selective in their acquisitions and thereby influence urban form and image as they go.

Gulf tastes tend toward buildings likely to be recognized as prestigious assets — with particular preference for world capitals' major landmarks, both old and new.

The process reinforces construction and maintenance of building icons, rather than projects that might contribute everyday amenities or gains for the urban public sphere.

Taste-based Assets

Qatar Investment Authority's (QIA) London portfolio includes the Canary Wharf business district and its landmark One Canada Square tower. QIA holds a 95% share of the Shard (the tallest building in Europe) and also owns the Porta Nuova business district in Milan, which includes the tallest building in Italy – the UniCredit Tower. Among New York's icons, QIA owns 10% of the Empire State Realty Trust.

London, 2015
The Shard from Southwark Bridge

Trophy buildings: their owners and their designers

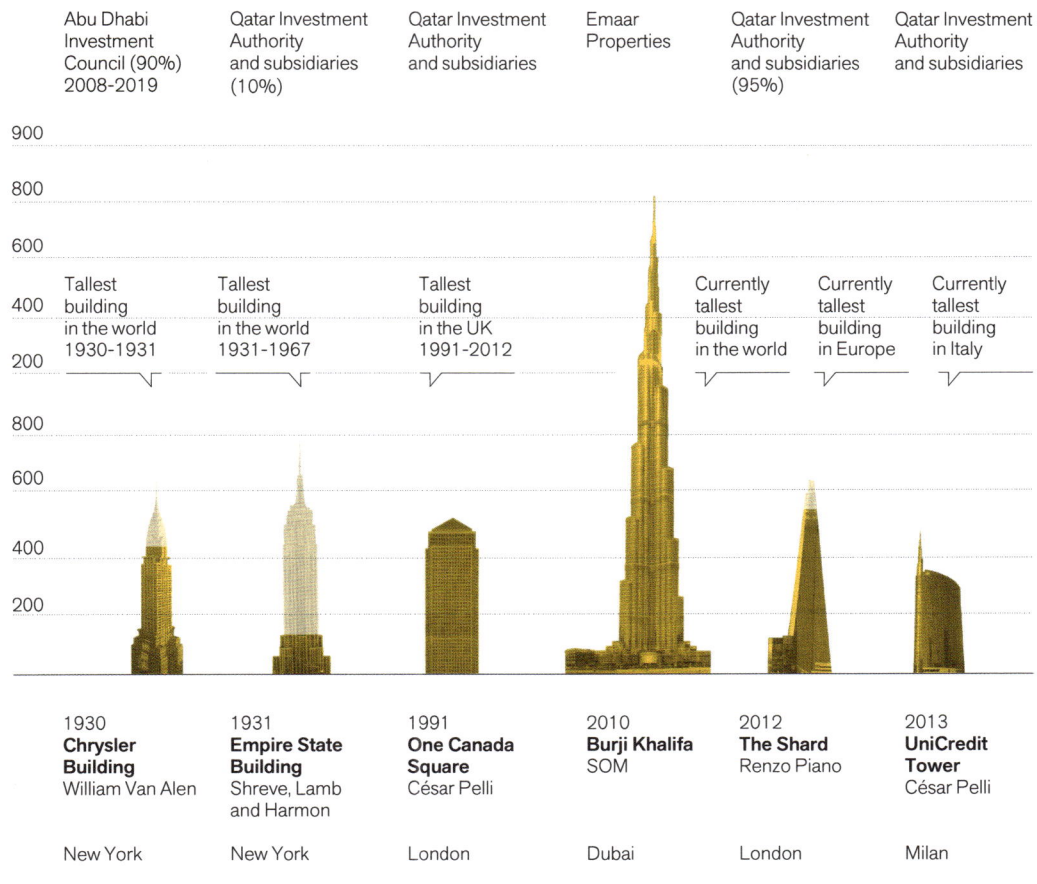

Qatar's Conspicuous Investments across the Planet

Qatar Investment Authority (QIA), along with its subsidiaries, has significant investment capacity – over US$300 billion. The map shows the group's geographical expansion that occurred from the mid-2000s to the mid-2010s. As with other Gulf wealth funds, ample cash flow allows purchases when property markets are low, with capacity of holding assets over the long term.

London, 2014
Canary Wharf and One Canada Square

Qatar Investment Authority holdings
(countries and number of properties)

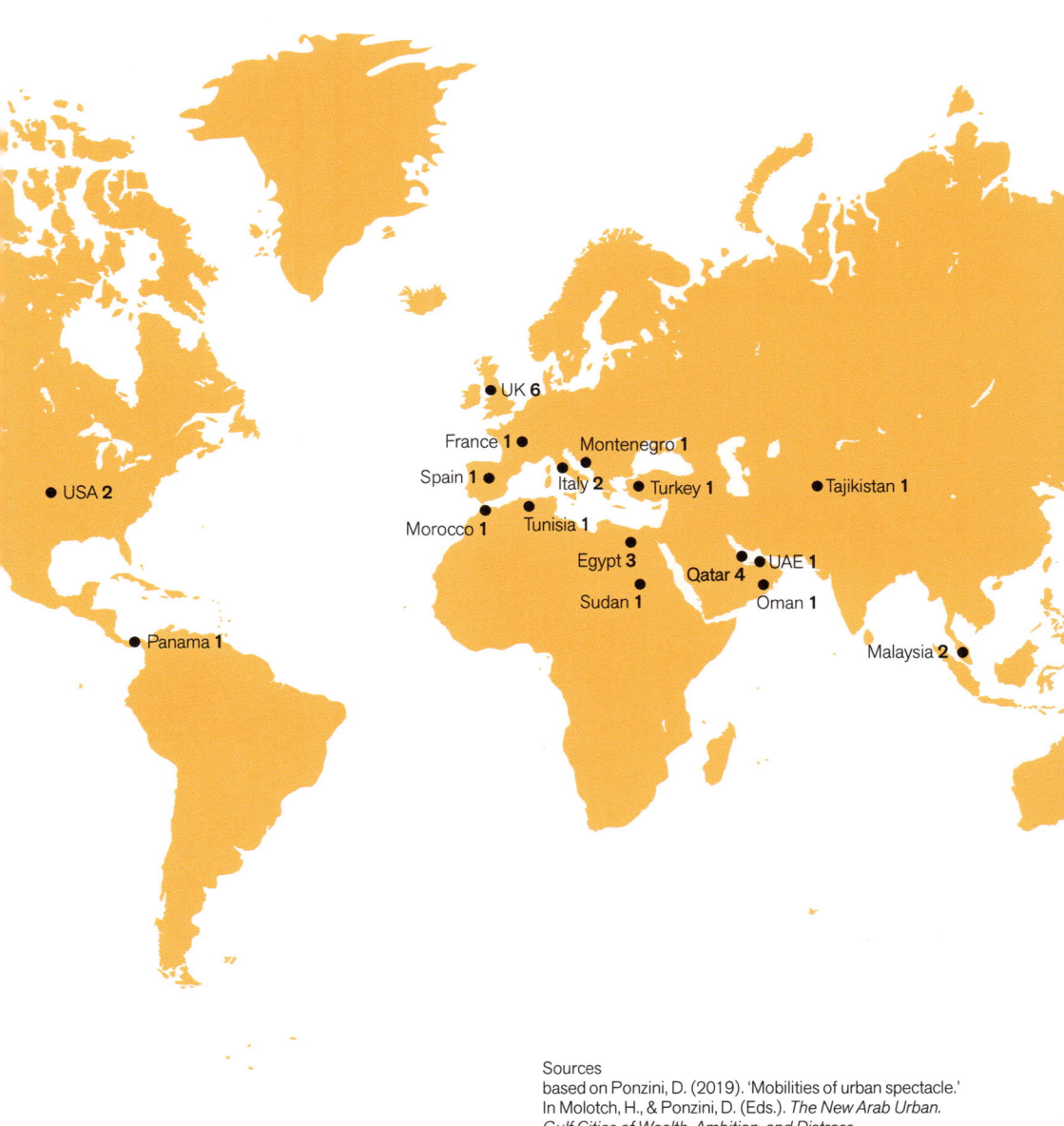

Sources
based on Ponzini, D. (2019). 'Mobilities of urban spectacle.'
In Molotch, H., & Ponzini, D. (Eds.). *The New Arab Urban. Gulf Cities of Wealth, Ambition, and Distress.*
New York: New York University Press, 79-96, p. 85;
www.qia.qa; www.qataridiar.com and others as of 2017

Homogenizing Building Lineups

Gulf-based taste helps fuel a zeal for distinctive shapes and forms in other parts of the globe. A short-sighted enthusiasm for flamboyance and recognizability may be leading to its own modes of urban homogenization – as in the cases of the geographically distant lineups of the City of London, Dubai's Business Bay, and Doha's West Bay (see pages 98-99).

Dubai, 2017
Business Bay

London, 2014
The City of London Seen from City Hall

At the Foot of the Icons

Even spectacular buildings, designed by world-class architects, can become pedestrian at their base. This is the case with both the London Shard and the Milan UniCredit Tower – landmarks designed respectively by Renzo Piano and César Pelli.

Owning such buildings adds luster to Qatar Investment Authority's asset portfolio and render its image noticeable across the world. However, as seen here, at the street level their iconic impressiveness is rather lessened.

London, 2015
St. Thomas Street and the Shard

Milan, 2021
UniCredit Tower
and Gae Aulenti Square

Abu Dhabi, 2017 (next pages)
Louvre Abu Dhabi

Modernization challenges local traditions and social institutions. Gulf cities deal with such tensions through spatial separation – of types of people, land uses, and modes of governance.

Spaces of Workaround

Allowing ports to host activities otherwise forbidden under Shari'a doctrine is consistent with other spatial demarcations to bypass administrative, social, or religious impediments. Designated tourist zones permit alcohol and other proscribed goods. Migrant workers live in particular city quarters or purpose-built camps on the urban outskirts. At the micro-level of a supermarket, pork products are restricted to separated rooms or enclosures.

Gulf cities' success in the Middle-East and the world depends, at least in part, on these spaces of workaround. They ease the way for Western notions of modernity to coexist with longer-standing local traditions of gender, vocation, and public dignity.

Abu Dhabi Workarounds

This map shows some of the locations, for Abu Dhabi, where otherwise problematic activities occur. Western cities, of course, have similar spaces of workarounds: tax-abatement zones and special planning precincts, illegal imigrant camps, de facto ghettos and red-light districts.
But they tend to be more informal in their origins, of smaller scale, and to develop from 'below' as well as from 'above.'

- Pork rooms
- Lounge/Cocktail bars
- Liquor stores

- Free zones
- Airports
- Major road
- Secondary road

Source
maps.google.com

0 — 5km

Paris, 2009
Louvre

The Place for Exception

Campuses for Western-style education enjoy social and gender mixing and a certain degree of academic freedom. The New York University Abu Dhabi campus is a case in point (see pages 16-17). For example, in the nearby Louvre Abu Dhabi museum – designed by French architect Jean Nouvel is itself a statement of openness to the West – nude statues are on display, bypassing the prohibition in most of the Gulf region.

Abu Dhabi, 2017
Louvre Abu Dhabi

Abu Dhabi, 2017 (next pages)
Louvre Abu Dhabi

Divided by Rules

Under conditions of vast increase in numbers of outsiders – tourists, workers, professionals, and students – modes of separation become still more ingenious. In Gulf cities as well as elsewhere, some such segregated zones are literally islands – as in the case of Abu Dhabi's special areas for cultural institutions on Saadiyat Island or the Abu Dhabi Global Market financial free zone on Al Maryah Island (see next pages).
In other cases, they are artificially demarcated – as in the case of the Dubai International Financial Centre and the Jebel Ali Free Zone, or the King Abdullah Financial Center in Riyadh. Modes of segregation, spatial fragmentation, and much else now replicate elsewhere.

Riyadh, 2017
King Abdullah Financial Center

Dubai, 2017
Dubai International Financial Center

Abu Dhabi, 2017 (next pages)
Global Market Square

Abu Dhabi, 2010
Corniche by Night

Afterword
From Trade Cities to Traded Cities in the Arabian Gulf

Nasser Rabbat
is the Aga Khan Professor and the Director of the Aga Khan Program for Islamic Architecture at MIT. He has published numerous articles and several books on topics ranging from Mamluk architecture to Antique Syria, nineteenth-century Cairo, and urbicide.

Editors' note:
In a speech launching our 2017 exhibition in Abu Dhabi, Nasser Rabbat expressed themes and understandings relevant not only to our own work but to intellectual issues across a wide range of potential inquiries. Displaying deep regional knowledge and of city-building more generally, Rabbat's analysis now serves as afterword to the current volume.

On the shore of malcontent, you sit, shadow bent down. You drink
Ocean water with a Coca Cola straw. And you drink the water
Of the Gulf. And you drink the sand of deserts. Alone, a stranger.
On the shore of creation, save for sorrow, oil, and Coca Cola!
Rainy clouds pass you by
Lift their gaze away from you… Withhold their rains off the seeds
Of devils in your heathen land.

Samih al-Qasem, *Sadder than Water*

There is a persistent correlation between the Orient and the fabulous in the Western mind. Not only the mysterious and mythical, but also the extraordinary and spectacular have animated a long history of imagining the Orient from the Ancient Greeks to the present. Herodotus claimed that Egypt was the source of the magical and spiritual knowledge that the Greeks absorbed and later developed: a view that was resurrected after the brief French occupation of Egypt at the end of the eighteenth century and the European rediscovery of the wonders of Ancient Egypt.

The Orient, too, was the locus of an existential foundational moment for the West with the emergence of Christianity in Palestine whence hailed not only Christ but also all of his apostles, as well as his parables and ethics, all tinged with a mysterious Oriental aura. That fabulous quality is most symbolically embodied in the Adoration of the Magis story. Guided by the Star of Bethlehem or the Star of the East, these wise men, who were most probably followers of the Persian prophet Zoroaster, visited the infant Jesus, recognized him as the coming Christ, and bore him precious presents: gold, frankincense, and myrrh, all items of wealth and luxury associated with the Orient and coveted by the West.

But the Magis story reflects a historical reality as well that goes back in time to the early records of civilization: the Orient was the emporium of luxury goods coming from near and far. Indeed, trade cities dotted the land between the Mediterranean and the Gulf and between Yemen and Anatolia and trade routes crossed the Arabian Peninsula and the Fertile Crescent connecting Asia to the Mediterranean and bringing the luxury goods of China, India, and Arabia to the consumption centers of Antiquity, first in Mesopotamia, Egypt, and Greece, and then Rome and Constantinople.

These Oriental cities, real and historical, became nonetheless subjects of myth, which heightened their extraordinary and spectacular attributes. The mythical narrative trumped history in articulating their image even after observation and documentation became the reliable tools of a new empirical method of representation in the nineteenth century. It even subsumed observation and documentation and turned them into reinforcements of the fantasies. Take for example Alfred de Musset (1810-1857), one of France's greatest poets, who says in his long poem, *Namouna, un conte oriental*,[1]

Consider too that I've stolen nothing
from the Bibliotheque; and that even though this story
is set in the Orient, I've said nothing about that.
It is true that I myself have never been there.
But it's so huge, so far away! – With memory,
We can claim what we want: go see it to believe it.
If, with a single brushstroke, I had built for you
Some blue-roofed town, some white mosques,
Some poetic outburst, plated in gold and silver,
Some description of a minaret flanked,
By a red horizon and assorted skies,
Would you have answered: 'Are you lying to me?'

1
Pages 316-17, de Musset, A. (1863). *Premières Poésies (1829-1835)*. Paris: Charpentier.
Considérez aussi que je n'ai rien volé
A la Bibliothèque; – et bien que cette histoire
Se passe en Orient, je n'en ai point parlé.
Il est vrai que, pour moi, je n'y suis point allé.
Mais c'est si grand, si loin! – Avec de la mémoire
On se tire de tout: – allez voir pour y croire.
Si d'un coup de pinceau je vous avais bâti
Quelque ville aux toits bleus, quelque blanche mosquée,
Quelque tirade en vers, d'or et d'argent plaquée,
Quelque description de minarets flanquée,
Avec l'horizon rouge et le ciel assorti,
M'auriez-vous répondu: 'Vous en avez menti?'

This image was so pervasive as to not only permeate literature, art, and the various emerging media of capitalism from Expositions Universelles, to advertisement and cinema, but also the actual urban projects in the Orient. Frank Lloyd Wright's romantic plan for Greater Baghdad in 1957-58, for instance, which comprised an opera house, museums, a zoo, and a university campus, is nothing less than an Oriental fantasy. Recalling the Round-city of Baghdad, built in the eighth century, the project came complete with an assortment of naïve references to what an American reared on the *One Thousand and One Nights* would have thought of the Orient. A hundred-meter tall, gilded statue of the Caliph Harun al-Rashid, the alleged Caliph of the Arabian Nights, was to be mounted on a spiraling base resembling the Malwiya Minaret at the ninth-century Mosque of al-Mutawakkil in Samarra to form the northern tip of the island complex. The opera house was to be decorated with scenes from the *Arabian Nights*, and its perforated dome wrapped around a statue of none other than Aladdin holding his lamp, in addition to two statues of Adam and Eve in the garden, symbolizing the Garden of Eden, all from the imagination of a master architect who implored local building professionals in a lecture he delivered in Baghdad to connect to 'what is deep in the spirit of the place.'

The blended heritage of fantasy and long-distance luxury trade reemerged forcefully after the oil boom in the late twentieth century Arabian Gulf. From Kuwait to Oman, new cities are rising out of the edge of the desert to amazing heights and vast expanses, with a concentration of high-rises that confidently competes with much larger cosmopolitan cities. Millennia later, these Arabian cities recovered the memory of their mercantile predecessors in Antiquity as loci of exchange, although their range of trading has expanded exponentially. It now encompasses the entire globe. Thus, the caravans and dhows of yesteryears have given way to slick world-class airports and airlines, highway networks, and gigantic seaports.

Kuwait City, 2017 (next pages)
Night View over Al Shaheed Park
and Sharq Skyline

Yet, the cities themselves are still negotiating a place between the desert and the sea, although contemporary engineering technologies, which have been exploited to an ecologically critical extreme, are allowing them to push the desert back and reclaim the sea in. Their swift expansion has thus been literally predicated upon their ability to equalize the two sharply distinct natural environments that have framed and defined them for so long, water and sand, and to mobilize them both in the service of super rapid and sometime drastic urbanization, fueled by the third natural element that they have in abundance: Oil.

Evidently there is an intermediate history stretching across long centuries between the fabled cities of Antiquity and the fantastic cities of today. This history has stamped the region with an austere Islamic character due to the looming desert beyond the horizon, yet also open to the influences coming from across the Persian Gulf, the Red Sea, and the faraway rims of the Indian Ocean. But it is also a history in which this region that gave Islam to the world had lain for centuries as ignored backwater on the periphery of larger empires whose capitals had been distant, careless, and occasionally harsh. This history left very few material traces, but its relentless hardship has carved deep burrows on the collective psyche of the people, which have not been totally washed out by the balm effect of the gushing oil. The sudden and immense prosperity engendered by oil in fact led to a paradoxical urbanity that exposed an uneasy mix of rentier economy, ruthless capitalism, ostentatious consumption, infrastructural sophistication, and cutting-edge technological contemporaneity coupled with a proud and tenacious traditionalism.

In the beginning, the pace of change was relatively restrained. The first discoveries of oil in the 1940s and 1950s and the unfair concessions imposed by multinational oil companies on rulers of the Gulf sheikhdoms brought in only modest wealth. The cities that have maintained the same patterns of traditional life and used the same types of vernacular architecture for centuries started to slowly acquire the basic amenities of modern life. New social and civic services were introduced, streets were cut across the traditional fabric or laid around it to service the new districts of apartment-buildings or separate villa-type residences, and new styles of urban living were thrust upon a population that had no prior experience of their underlying and totally foreign social adjustments.

Things changed more spectacularly in the wake of the mid-1970s oil price boom: the Gulf cities-states suddenly became super-rich. With the massive cash flow and its concomitant economic empowerment came the desire to develop fast and big. The cities expanded rapidly, with all the amenities of modern living and up to date infrastructure installed in record time to accommodate the growing population of native and expatriates and to satisfy their newly acquired expensive tastes. A fervent quest for cultural identity combined with the accumulating wealth generated a demand for contemporary, yet recognizably local architecture. Sincerely at times, but opportunistically at others, architects responded by incorporating in their otherwise state-of-the-art designs historical elements dubbed 'traditional,' 'Arabic,' or 'Islamic,' depending on the preferences of the patrons. But, as anthropologist Ahmed Kanna pointed out, this top-down hurried urbanization was nonetheless imagined as a white European elitist utopia.[2]

[2] Page 24, Kanna, A. (2011). *Dubai, the City as Corporation.* Minneapolis: University of Minnesota Press.

The grand project of expansion is still going on despite short halts caused by a series of international or regional crises. The Gulf cities in fact recently grew by leaps and bounds under the dual influence of a long-brewing geopolitical rivalry and a sudden and unprecedented terrorist act. The decisive victory of the West against the Soviet block in 1989 emboldened an already rampant and multinational neo-Capitalism to further extend its search for new and profitable outlets. The Gulf, awash in cash, relatively under-exploited, and eager to diversify and secure its sources of income presented the perfect combination of willing market and potential partner to global business.

The investment opportunities became even more localized after the 9/11 terrorist attacks. Erratic new financial and security measures in the West, ostensibly aimed at fighting terrorism, instigated a partial reorientation of the accumulated Gulf wealth in international financial institutions. Some of it began to head back to the Gulf cities to join the resident wealth in real-estate development as the easiest and most reliable investment. Architecture at once assumed the role of branding instrument and spectacular wrapping for these new lavish enterprises, which swiftly sprang up in all the major cities and broke all previous measures of scale, form, luxury, and, at time, urban vision.

Dubai, with its entrepreneurial spirit, unrestrained economic laisser-faire policies, and aggressive pursuit of investments, was the first to ride the new tide and guide it. The entire city, its surrounding desert, and even its coastal water became the World's most phenomenal visual laboratory where the only check on urban flights of fancy seems to be the unbridled ability of the designers to push the limits of size, height, eccentricity, dominance over the environment, and desire, and the willingness of their patrons to bankroll those fantasies with little regard to their potential ecological and social costs.

In this make-believe milieu, the architecture of what Mike Davis called the 'utopian capitalist city' has emerged as a tacit design objective shared by the designers and their patrons to lure in more investors in a financial cyclical scheme that seems to have recovered most of its steam after the crash of 2008. Thoughtful modernism, regionalism, traditionalism, revivalism, and even postmodernism have been hastily given up in favor of a new extravagant architecture that loudly, and often too loudly, bespeaks the ambition to endow a global pursuit of luxury aimed at the super-wealthy jet-setters with a fabulous Oriental imagery that Joseph Rykwert matter-of-factly called the 'Emirate Style.'[3]

The Dubai Syndrome spread to other cities in the Gulf, and beyond into the major cities of neighboring countries that cannot sustain this kind of financial, urban, or social extravaganza. The syndrome usually manifests itself in two variations, which are sometimes combined in one: super-slick high-rises competing to cut a particular, futuristic profile above the skyline of the city, or an exclusive

[3] Pages 370-71, Rykwert, J. (2008). *The Judicious Eye: Architecture Against the Other Arts.* Chicago: Chicago University Press.

excursion down some gilded memory lane of an imaginary *Arabian Nights*-inspired Oriental splendor.

Some Gulf cities are trying to taper the seemingly unstoppable Dubai effect by investing in culture and education as counterparts to the naked commercialism of business and luxury towers and cavernous malls, and as long-term enrichment projects in preparation for the after the oil economy. But these projects, however ambitious, have yet to identify their audience, respond to their expectations, and build their pedagogical, cultural and/or social missions on clear footing. As of now, many of the completed museums and sleek universities' campuses are underperforming while a number are still just shimmering images blipping on the computer screens of scores of swooning potential patrons, architects, and students of architecture around the world. Most were deliberately commissioned from international starchitects as a way to encapsulate the glamour associated with these world-famous designers in the actual buildings they design. They were perhaps meant to tacitly present the sensational envelope as the aspiration — and potentially the substitute for — the still unclear content and unresolved tensions embedded in the scale, extravagance, and ambiguous social, cultural, and pedagogical functions of the buildings themselves.

The reasons for this state of affairs are many. Some are socio-political and can be summed up by two complementary questions: what do the patrons in the Gulf, namely the ruling sheikhs and their families and business partners, want their cities to be and why? And how does the population comprehend theses intentions and react to them? Other reasons have to do with the profession of architecture and planning and its changing conceptual, financial, technical, and ethical parameters, which are affecting the way in which architects see themselves and evaluate their role and the meaning of their work. Still others are purely economic: they relate to the effects of the insatiable but lazy late capitalism, which animates most investments in the Gulf (and the entire world for that matter) today. Most of these issues have been dissected in numerous publications, but very few have managed to advance a historically grounded perspective.

One factor that has not received much attention in the current discourse, however, has to do with the deep historical roots of the Gulf cities. Although spectacle and excess are clearly predicated on contemporary socioeconomic factors, the culture of exchange inherited through millennia affects the kind and choice of architecture in the Arabian Gulf cities today in similar ways to how it did in the past. It is also, conversely, bolstered by the success of that architecture. But having focused on one specific kind of trade, namely real-estate and its accouterments, the Gulf cities have turned into cities of trade in an existential sense: the object of trade has become the city itself, its image, its potential, and its inviting glitzy buildings that function mostly as billboards for the urban brand. That outcome is the not-so-hidden price that the Gulf cities are paying for having transformed themselves from trade cities to traded cities.

Another price that the expansion and hyper commercialization are exacting poses a more direct ethical dilemma: how to treat imported labor? The relentless urbanization needed a huge labor force to sustain it, which the native Gulfis could not or would not provide. A massive and quite discriminatory process of importing poor labor mostly from South and Southeast Asia ensued, through which hundreds of thousands of disenfranchised workers were brought to run all of the services in the Arabian cities, and build their infra and supra structures under extreme conditions. Lodged in crowded and ill-kempt camps and rental neighborhoods, these workers epitomize the urban and social imbalance that many developing cities in the world suffered from in the postcolonial period with the flight of the bourgeoisie from their old centers and their replacement by poor rural immigration. Like the rural migrants in the old colonial cities, the workers in the Arabian cities are poor, unskilled, and unaccustomed to city life. But unlike the rural migrants of yesteryears the workers in the Gulf are actually foreign. They share neither language nor culture with the native privileged population or with the professional expatriates, who come mostly from the West.

Nor are these workers granted any civic or political rights in their host countries. The severe problems that this situation has created have yet to be legislatively tackled although signs of relenting to international pressure are showing up with the Gulf governments promising to ease the restrictions that have shackled their guest workers. Not surprisingly, the situation is paradoxical, as the Gulf cities force their ways into the contemporary world of business and finance and glitzy architecture, but maintain a medieval form of labor relations. One way to solve this dilemma is to recognize the rights of imported workers as city citizens. For if national citizenship is impossible for the millions of expats because of demographic fears among the natives, then a city citizenship, promulgating a set of rights to the city and its spaces, would allow all the inhabitants of the city to have similar privileges and responsibilities within its administrative boundaries. The ontological dimension of belonging: blood, language, religion, tribalism, can remain exclusive at the level of national identity, thus alleviating the natives' anxiety. But this, I conclude, is a proposition that has to come from within the Gulf civic societies.

Riyadh, 2017 (next pages)
King Fahad National Library Park

Appendix
Post-its from the Gulf

We join with others to keep looking for further links between Gulf cities and other cities, as transnational connectivity keeps changing in pattern and extent. The Gulf cases invite shifts in imagining the kinds and ways of learning we can collectively advance.

An example to the rest of the world! They have achieved what others have attempted to in no time at all. All we want to know is what's next?

When they run out of oil...

Abu Dhabi 2015

New York 2016

Gulf City Researching and Learning Processes

The materials in this book derive from the 'Learning from Gulf Cities' initiative – a series of events in Abu Dhabi, New York, and Milan. Accompanying photographic exhibitions invited viewers to indicate, with the simple device of post-its, their questions and concerns about what they were seeing. We gained thoughts about the Gulf in relation to other parts of the world, as well as anxieties about how risky Gulf city models might be for other cities to follow. The New York and Abu Dhabi exhibition openings (respectively in 2016 and 2017) included keynote speeches, one by Amale Andraos and one by Nasser Rabbat.

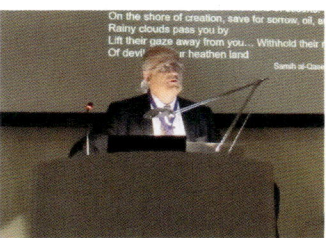

Milan 2017 **Abu Dhabi 2017**

1
Stop trying to be like another city. Be the Gulf.

2
Isn't it far more interesting to walk these streets than to drive down them, even though Gulf cities weren't built for walking. So much more to be experienced at street level. I find every other vantage point to be deceptive.

3
Gulf cities shouldn't be used as models as they are built around an obsolete car-centric ideal. Unless Gulf Cities switch from cars to people, they still have a lot of progress to go through before being examples to the whole world. Gulf cities fail to capture the livability, walkability and overall feel of belonging and wonderlust that many European cities have. Gulf cities, for now, feel empty yet full of buildings and lonely yet full of people.

4
Stop building cities that make me feel like I'm in the Truman Show.

5
Think about the aesthetics from the ground, not the sky.

Doha, 2017 (next pages)
Friday at the Mosque of the Qatar
Faculty of Islamic Studies

Learning from Gulf Cities: Spectacles, Investments, Buildings

Exhibition and Event Space, NYUAD New York
March 28 – April 15, 2016

Curators and Coordinators
Harvey Molotch
New York University
Davide Ponzini
Politecnico di Milano

Photography
Michele Nastasi
Università Ca' Foscari Venezia

Exhibition Design
Argot ou La Maison Mobile
Luca Astorri
Riccardo Balzarotti
Rossella Locatelli
Matteo Poli
Politecnico di Milano
with
Caterina Dicorato
and Matteo Lazzari

Research Assistants
Fabio Manfredini
Politecnico di Milano
Martha Coe
New York University
Maryam Karimi
Politecnico di Milano
Liana Mandradzhieva
Politecnico di Milano

Infographics by
Argot ou La Maison Mobile
and Department
of Architecture
and Urban Studies
of Politecnico di Milano

With Support from
New York University
Abu Dhabi Institute
NYU Institute for Public Knowledge
Department of Architecture and Urban Studies of Politecnico di Milano

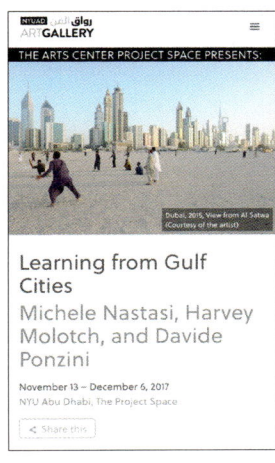

Learning from Gulf Cities

NYUAD Art Gallery
November 13 – December 6, 2017

Curators and Coordinators
Harvey Molotch
New York University
Davide Ponzini
Politecnico di Milano

Photography
Michele Nastasi
Università Ca' Foscari Venezia

Exhibition Design
**Argot ou La Maison Mobile
Luca Astorri
Riccardo Balzarotti
Rossella Locatelli
Matteo Poli**
Politecnico di Milano
Celeste Calzolari
Politecnico di Milano
Michele Nastasi
Università Ca' Foscari Venezia

Research Assistants
Mina Akhavan
Politecnico di Milano
Celeste Calzolari
Politecnico di Milano
Martha Coe
New York University
Anita De Franco
Politecnico di Milano
Zachary Jones
Politecnico di Milano
Maryam Karimi
Politecnico di Milano
Liana Mandradzhieva
Politecnico di Milano
Fabio Manfredini
Politecnico di Milano

Infographics by
**Argot ou La Maison Mobile
and Department
of Architecture
and Urban Studies
of Politecnico di Milano**

With Support from
**NYUAD Institute
NYU Institute for Public Knowledge
The NYU Abu Dhabi Art Gallery
Akkasah Center
for Photography, NYUAD
Department of Architecture
and Urban Studies
of Politecnico di Milano**

1
Is the Gulf City ahead or the last?
2
Very good question!

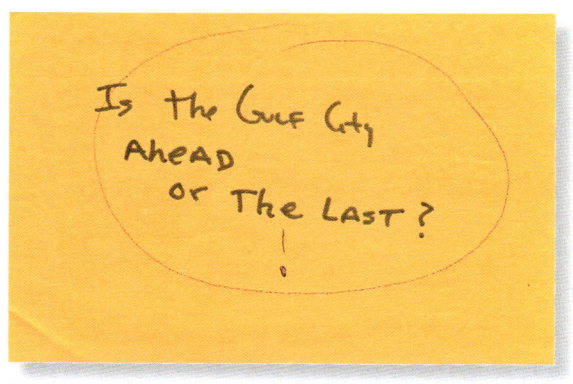

1

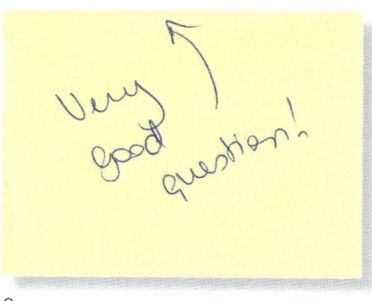

2

Abu Dhabi, 2015
Michele's Seeing through

References

See the Gulf, See the World

Boodrookas, A., & Keshavarzian, A. (2019). 'Giving the transnational a history: Gulf cities across time and space.' In Molotch, H., & Ponzini, D. (Eds.). *The New Arab Urban. Gulf Cities of Wealth, Ambition, and Distress*. New York: New York University Press, 35-57.

Bouman, O., Khoubrou, M., & Koolhaas, R. (2007, Eds.). *Al Manakh*. Amsterdam: Stichting Archis.

Molotch, H., & Ponzini, D. (2019). 'Introduction: Learning from Gulf cities.' In Id. (Eds.). *The New Arab Urban. Gulf Cities of Wealth, Ambition, and Distress*. New York: New York University Press, 1-31.

Reisz, T. (2010, Ed.). *Al Manakh 2 Cont'd*. Amsterdam: Stichting Archis.

Szelenyi, I. (2017). 'Pakistani guest workers in the United Arab Emirates.' *Demografia*, 59(5), 5-47.

City Icons for the World

Alawadi, K. (2018, Ed.). *Lifescapes beyond Bigness*. London: Artifice.

Elsheshtawy, Y. (2009). *Dubai: Behind an Urban Spectacle*. London: Routledge.

Nastasi, M. (2019). 'A Gulf of images: Photography and the circulation of spectacular architecture.' In Molotch, H., & Ponzini, D. (Eds.). *The New Arab Urban. Gulf Cities of Wealth, Ambition, and Distress*. New York: New York University Press, 99-129.

Tourist City as Hub

Molotch, H. (2019). 'Consuming Abu Dhabi.' In Molotch, H., & Ponzini, D. (Eds.). *The New Arab Urban. Gulf Cities of Wealth, Ambition, and Distress*. New York: New York University Press, 256-275.

Sharpley, R. (2008). 'Planning for tourism: The case of Dubai.' *Tourism and Hospitality Planning & Development*, 5(1), 13-30.

Buildings Travel

Lowry, G., & McCann, E. (2011). 'Asia in the mix: Urban form and global mobilities – Hong Kong, Vancouver, Dubai.' In Roy, A., & Ong, A. (Eds.). *Worlding Cities. Asian Experiments and the Art of Being Global*. Chichester: Blackwell-Wiley, 182–204.

Ponzini, D. (2020). *Transnational Architecture and Urbanism: Rethinking How Cities Plan, Transform, and Learn*. London: Routledge.

Landmarks Can't Travel

Ponzini, D., & Arosio, P. M. (2017). 'Urban effects of the transnational circulation of branded buildings: Comparing two skyscrapers and their context in Barcelona and Doha.' *Urban Design International*, 22(1), 28-46.

Salama, A. M., & Wiedmann, F. (2013). *Demystifying Doha: On Architecture and Urbanism in an Emerging City*. Adelshot: Ashgate.

Testing and Spreading

Ibrahim, S. (2020). *Dubai: La Genèse d'un Modèle Extrême dans le Circuit des Villes Globales*. PhD Thesis, Paris Est University.

Wippel, S., Bromber, K., & Krawietz, B. (2016, Eds.). *Under Construction: Logics of Urbanism in the Gulf Region*. London: Routledge.

Collecting Trophy Buildings

Ponzini, D. (2019). 'Mobilities of urban spectacle: Plans, projects, and investments in the Gulf and beyond.' In Molotch, H., & Ponzini, D. (Eds.). *The New Arab Urban. Gulf Cities of Wealth, Ambition, and Distress*. New York: New York University Press, 79-96.

Hertog, S. (2019). 'A quest for significance: Gulf oil monarchies' international strategies and their urban dimensions.' In Molotch, H., & Ponzini, D. (Eds.). *The New Arab Urban. Gulf Cities of Wealth, Ambition, and Distress*. New York: New York University Press, 276-299.

Spaces of Workaround

Easterling, K. (2014). *Extrastatecraft. The Power of Infrastructure Space*. New York: Verso Books.

Keshavarzian, A. (2010). 'Geopolitics and the genealogy of free trade zones in the Persian Gulf.' *Geopolitics*, 15(2), 263-289.

Molotch, H., & Ponzini, D. (2019). 'Conclusion: From Gulf cities onward.' In Id. (Eds.). *The New Arab Urban. Gulf Cities of Wealth, Ambition, and Distress*. New York: New York University Press, 300-321.

Acknowledgments

We thank our two home institutions, New York University and Politecnico di Milano, for their continuous support. At NYU, the Abu Dhabi Institute was a critical financial and organizational resource. In addition, the NYUAD Akkasah Center for Photography provided a grant for Nastasi's 2017 Gulf photographic field work; the NYUAD Art Gallery supported our 2017 exhibition, 'Learning from Gulf Cities.'

At Politecnico di Milano, the Department of Architecture and Urban Studies provided additional financial, editorial, and logistical assistance for the 2016 and 2017 exhibitions as well as for completing the materials used for this book. We thank them all for making these projects possible.

Along the way, we have collaborated with many exceptional colleagues and assistants, some of whom have given us expert commentaries on our previous papers and publications. We would like to thank them for their generous help. In addition, we acknowledge once again the late Hilary Ballon, former NYU Deputy Vice-Chancellor for Abu Dhabi and NYU University Professor, for her vital intellectual engagement and leadership.

SEEING THROUGH GULF CITIES
URBANIZATION IN AND FROM THE ARABIAN PENINSULA

Authored by
Harvey Molotch, Davide Ponzini
with Michele Nastasi (Photography)

Afterword by
Nasser Rabbat

Research Assistance
Zachary M. Jones

Copy Editing
Barclay Gail Swerling

Editorial Director
Alessandro Martinelli

Published by
ListLab
info@listlab.eu
listlab.eu

Graphic Design
Roberto Libanori

Art Director & Production
Blacklist Creative, BCN
blacklist-creative.com

ISBN 9788832080728

**Printed and bound
in the European Union**, 2022

series

All rights reserved
© of ListLab edition;
© of the author's texts;
© of the author's images;

No part of this book may be reproduced, stored in a retrieval system, or transmitted in any form or by any means, including electronic, mechanical, photocopying, microfilming, recording, or otherwise without written permission from the publisher.

Sales, Marketing & Distribution
distribution@listlab.eu
listlab.eu/en/distribuzione/

ListLab Scientific Commission
Massimiliano Scaglione (ListLab CEO);
Alessandro Martinelli (ListLab Editor-in-Chief);
Eve Blau; Fabrizio Bozzato; Maurizio Carta;
Elisa Cattaneo; Lawrence C. Davis; Antonio De Rossi;
Santiago Del Hierro; Marcella Del Signore;
Corrado Diamantini; Raffaella Fagnoni;
Carlo Gasparrini; Manuel Gausa; Michael Jakob;
Lorenzo Imbesi; Monica Kuo; Giuseppe Losco;
John Palmesino; Patrizia Ranzo; Mosè Ricci;
Massimo Sargolini; Jörg Schröder; Chiara Sonzogni;
Maria Chiara Tosi; Manolo Ufer.

For more information about the Editorial Board and Scientific Commission, please visit:
listlab.eu/en/board

ListLab was established in 2007 and has elaborated on the idea of an international editorial laboratory with a multidisciplinary approach to architecture, planning, arts, photography, and design. List Group, found in 2021, aims at creating networks and promoting debates and cultural exchange, but also organize events from which new knowledge about architecture, cities, and landscape can develop. Today, List Group is composed of **ListLab**, the publishing house, **Blacklist**, the graphic design studio, **Instaura**, the informational weblog, and **Us/Them/Yours**, a creative agency that aims at a multimedia approach to information.